JUSTICE
AND THE
WAR ON
TERROR

JEWISH LEARNING INSTITUTE

ACCREDITED FOR ATTORNEYS

CLE

* In some states

Course Development

Rabbi Mordechai Dinerman
Rabbi Shmuel Klatzkin, PhD
Rabbi Eli Raksin
Menachem Sandman, Esq.
Rabbi Naftali Silberberg

Printed in the United States of America
© Published and Copyrighted 2014 by
The Rohr Jewish Learning Institute
822 Eastern Parkway, Brooklyn, NY 11213

(888) YOUR-JLI/718-221-6900
www.myJLI.com

ב"ה

The **Rohr Jewish Learning Institute**
gratefully acknowledges
the pioneering support of

George and Pamela Rohr

SINCE ITS INCEPTION,
the **Rohr JLI** has been
a beneficiary of the vision, generosity,
care, and concern
of the **Rohr family**

In the merit of
the tens of thousands of hours of Torah study
by **JLI** students worldwide,
may they be blessed with health,
Yiddishe nachas from all their loved ones,
and extraordinary success
in all their endeavors

TABLE OF CONTENTS

JUSTICE AND THE WAR ON TERROR

The Hostage Dilemma

In 2011, Israel set 1,027 prisoners free in exchange for the release of Gilad Shalit. More recently, the rise of ISIS and the murders of James Foley, Steven Sotloff, Peter Kassig, and Luke Somers have forced us to revisit this difficult debate: Should we pay sizable ransoms or release dangerous criminals in exchange for the life and freedom of an innocent hostage?

JLI

JEWISH LEARNING INSTITUTE

Two Hostages, Two Outcomes

Text 1

James Foley, quoted in Terrence McCoy, "James Foley's Last Message to His Family: 'I Am Going to Need Your Help to Reclaim My Life,'" *Washington Post*, Aug. 25, 2014

Dear Family and Friends,

I remember going to the Mall with Dad, a very long bike ride with Mom. I remember so many great family times that take me away from this prison. Dreams of family and friends take me away and happiness fills my heart.

I know you are thinking of me and praying for me. And I am so thankful. I feel you all especially when I pray. I pray for you to stay strong and to believe. I really feel I can touch you even in this darkness when I pray.

Eighteen of us have been held together in one cell, which has helped me. We have had each other to have endless long conversations about movies, trivia, sports. We have played games made up of scraps found in our cell . . . we have found ways to play checkers, Chess, and Risk . . . and have had tournaments of competition, spending some days preparing strategies for the next day's game or lecture. The games and teaching each other have helped the time pass. They have been a huge help. We repeat stories and laugh to break the tension.

I have had weak and strong days. We are so grateful when anyone is freed; but of course, yearn for our own freedom. We try to encourage each other and share strength. We are being fed better now and daily. We have tea, occasional coffee. I have regained most of my weight lost last year.

I think a lot about my brothers and sister. I remember playing Werewolf in the dark with Michael and so many other adventures. I think of chasing Mattie and T around the kitchen counter. It makes me happy to think of them. If there is any money left in my bank account, I want it to go to Michael and Matthew. I am so proud of you, Michael, and thankful to you for happy childhood memories and to you and Kristie for happy adult ones.

And big John, how I enjoyed visiting you and Cress in Germany. Thank you for welcoming me. I think a lot about RoRo and try to imagine what Jack is like. I hope he has RoRo's personality!

And Mark . . . so proud of you, too, Bro. I think of you on the West Coast and hope you are doing some snowboarding and camping, I especially remember us going to the Comedy Club in Boston together and our big hug after. The special moments keep me hopeful.

Katie, so very proud of you. You are the strongest and best of us all!! I think of you working so hard, helping people as a nurse. I am so glad we texted just before I was captured. I pray I can come to your wedding. . . . now I am sounding like Grammy!!

Grammy, please take your medicine, take walks and keep dancing. I plan to take you out to Margarita's when I get home. Stay strong because I am going to need your help to reclaim my life.

Jim

Rukmini Callimachi, "Before Killing James Foley, ISIS Demanded Ransom from U.S.," *New York Times*, Aug. 20, 2014

Kneeling in the dirt in a desert somewhere in the Middle East, James Foley lost his life this week at the hands of the Islamic State in Iraq and Syria. Before pulling out the knife used to decapitate him, his masked executioner explained that he was killing the 40-year-old American journalist in retaliation for the recent United States' airstrikes against the terrorist group in Iraq.

In fact, until recently, ISIS had a very different list of demands for Mr. Foley: The group pressed the United States to provide a multimillion-dollar ransom for his release, according to a representative of his family and a former hostage held alongside him. The United States—unlike several European countries that have funneled millions to the terror group to spare the lives of their citizens—refused to pay. . . .

Along with the three Americans, ISIS is holding citizens of Britain, which like the United States has declined to pay ransoms, former hostages confirmed. The terror group has sent a laundry list of demands for the release of the foreigners, starting with money but also prisoner swaps, including the liberation of Aafia Siddiqui, an M.I.T.-trained Pakistani neuroscientist with ties to Al Qaeda currently incarcerated in Texas.

The policy of not making concessions to terrorists and not paying ransoms has put the United States and Britain at odds with other European allies, which have routinely paid significant sums to win the release of their citizens—including four French and three Spanish hostages who were released this year after money was delivered through an intermediary, according to two of the victims and their colleagues.

Kidnapping Europeans has become the main source of revenue for Al Qaeda and its affiliates, which have earned at least $125 million in ransom payments in the past five years alone, according to an investigation by The Times. Although ISIS was recently expelled from Al Qaeda and abides by different rules, recently freed prisoners said that their captors were well aware of what ransoms had been paid on behalf of European citizens held by Qaeda affiliates as far afield as Africa, indicating that they were hoping to abide by the same business plan.

QUESTIONS FOR DISCUSSION

1. Should governments pay ransoms in order to secure the release of their citizens?

2. Would you distinguish between paying ransoms and releasing terror suspects or convicts? Why?

Legal Analysis

The Federal Material Support Statute

Text 3

Dion Nissenbaum, et al., "James Foley's Killing Highlights Debate over Ransom," *Wall Street Journal*, Aug. 22, 2014

Until the day American journalist James Foley was killed by Sunni extremists in the Middle East, his family and friends were working to collect millions of dollars they hoped would secure his freedom.

They knew they couldn't raise the $123 million his captors had demanded. But they were still hopeful they could collect $5 million to offer for Mr. Foley's release. . . .

The effort to raise a ransom for Mr. Foley faced another obstacle: The U.S. government considers such payments illegal funding of terrorist organizations.

During the course of Mr. Foley's captivity, the Federal Bureau of Investigation discouraged the family from paying a ransom because of concerns that paying money fuels the kidnapping industry, said one Justice Department official.

Text 4

The Federal Material Support Statute, Federal Code 18 U.S.C. § 2339B(a)(1)

Whoever knowingly provides material support or resources to a foreign terrorist organization, or attempts or conspires to do so, shall be fined under this title or imprisoned not more than 15 years, or both, and, if the death of any person results, shall be imprisoned for any term of years or for life. To violate this paragraph, a person must have knowledge that the organization is a designated terrorist organization (as defined in subsection (g)(6)), that the organization has engaged or engages in terrorist activity (as defined in section 212(a)(3)(B) of the Immigration and Nationality Act), or that the organization has engaged or engages in terrorism (as defined in section 140(d)(2) of the Foreign Relations Authorization Act, Fiscal Years 1988 and 1989).

Text 5

Shannon Chapla, "ND Expert: Illegal Ransom Payments Principal Source of ISIS Funding," *Notre Dame News*, Aug. 22, 2014, www.news.nd.edu/

Collecting ransom payments is a principal source of funding for ISIS, according to terrorist financing expert Jimmy Gurulé, professor of law at the University of Notre Dame, who says making such a payment is a federal crime.

"ISIS and other foreign terrorist groups have raised hundreds of millions of dollars from the collection of ransom payments," says Gurulé, also a former assistant U.S. attorney general and former undersecretary for enforcement for the U.S. Treasury Department. "Under the federal material support statute, the payment of funds to a 'foreign terrorist organization' is federal crime punishable by a maximum term of 15 years in prison."

Gurulé says there is no kidnapping or humanitarian exception to this statute.

"Any payment of funds to a foreign terrorist organization, regardless of the donor's intent, is a federal felony," he says.

QUESTION FOR DISCUSSION

Should there be a kidnapping or humanitarian exception to the material support statute?

The "Necessity" Defense

Text 6a

State v. Warshow, 1979 138 Vt. 22, 410 A.2d 1000, (1979)

The defense of necessity is one that partakes of the classic defense of "confession and avoidance." It admits the criminal act, but claims justification....

The doctrine is one of specific application insofar as it is a defense to criminal behavior. This is clear because if the qualifications for the defense of necessity are not closely delineated, the definition of criminal activity becomes uncertain and even whimsical. The difficulty arises when words of general and broad qualification are used to describe the special scope of this defense.

In the various definitions and examples recited as incorporating the concept of necessity, certain fundamental requirements stand out:

(1) there must be a situation of emergency arising without fault on the part of the actor concerned;

(2) this emergency must be so imminent and compelling as to raise a reasonable expectation of harm, either directly to the actor or upon those he was protecting;

(3) this emergency must present no reasonable opportunity to avoid the injury without doing the criminal act; and

(4) the injury impending from the emergency must be of sufficient seriousness to outmeasure the criminal wrong.

Text 6b

Commonwealth v. Jeb E. Brugmann, 13 Mass. App. Ct. 373 (1982)

The application of the defense is limited to the following circumstances:

(1) the defendant is faced with a clear and imminent danger, not one which is debatable or speculative;

(2) the defendant can reasonably expect that his action will be effective as the direct cause of abating the danger;

(3) there is no legal alternative which will be effective in abating the danger; and

(4) the Legislature has not acted to preclude the defense by a clear and deliberate choice regarding the values at issue.

LEARNING EXERCISE

If someone who paid a ransom is prosecuted for providing material support to a terror organization, would the case have the "fundamental requirements" for a "necessity defense"?

State v. Warshow, 1979 138 Vt. 22, 410 A.2d 1000, (1979)

	Requirement	Applicable	Inapplicable
1.	Emergency without fault		
2.	Reasonable expectation of harm		
3.	No opportunity to avoid		
4.	Sufficient seriousness to outmeasure the wrong		

Commonwealth v. Jeb E. Brugmann, 13 Mass. App. Ct. 373 (1982)

	Requirement	Applicable	Inapplicable
1.	Clear and imminent danger		
2.	Reasonable expectation that the action will be effective		
3.	No legal alternative		
4.	Legislature has not made a clear and deliberate choice		

Text 7

Jens David Ohlin, "Ransom and Material Support,"
www.opiniojuris.org, Sep. 18, 2014

Necessity is often excluded as a defense if the statutory provision embodies a specific legislative choice or policy to criminalize the decision made by the defendant. However . . . there is no evidence that Congress had in mind the specific situation of paying ransom to terrorists. If, in the future, Congress passes a specific statute outlawing the paying of ransom to terrorists by private citizens, then the exclusion would be relevant.

C. Duress

Text 8

United States v. Bailey, 444 U.S. 394, 410 (1980)

Common law historically distinguished between the defenses of duress and necessity. Duress was said to excuse criminal conduct where the actor was under an unlawful threat of imminent death or serious bodily injury, which threat caused the actor to engage in conduct violating the literal terms of the criminal law. While the defense of duress covered the situation where the coercion had its source in the actions of other human beings, the defense of necessity, or choice of evils, traditionally covered the situation where physical forces beyond the actor's control rendered illegal conduct the lesser of two evils. Thus, where A destroyed a dike because B threatened to kill him if he did not, A would argue that he acted under duress; whereas if A destroyed the dike in order to protect more valuable property from flooding, A could claim a defense of necessity.

Text 9

Jens David Ohlin, "Ransom and Material Support," www.opiniojuris.org, Sep. 18, 2014

Necessity applies when a defendant, in response to a threat or emergency, violates a criminal prohibition because doing so represents the lesser of two evils. In that sense, the necessity defense has a utilitarian or consequentialist logic stemming from its status as a justification. If the defendant produces a greater evil, then the defense no longer applies.

In contrast, duress applies when the defendant performs a criminal act due to a threat of grave injury or death to the defendant or a close associate, emanating from a third party. . . . The paradigm of duress involves an autonomy-reducing threat that requires a level of moral heroism that cannot be expected by the law. The third party "forces" the defendant to violate the criminal prohibition by virtue of a threat that cannot be reasonably ignored. As such, duress is an excuse which negates the culpability of the actor. As an excuse, duress should not require that the defendant selected the lesser of two evils, because the claim has nothing to do with the defendant's selection of a better outcome.

Talmudic Analysis

A Rabbinic Enactment

Text 10a

Mishnah, Gitin 4:6

Mishnah

The first authoritative work of Jewish law that was codified in writing. The Mishnah contains the oral traditions that were passed down from teacher to student; it supplements, clarifies, and systematizes the commandments of the Torah. Due to the continual persecution of the Jewish people, it became increasingly difficult to guarantee that these traditions would not be forgotten. Rabbi Yehudah Hanasi therefore redacted the Mishnah at the end of the 2nd century. It serves as the foundation for the Talmud.

אין פודין את השבויים יתר על דמיהן, מפני תיקון העולם.

For the purpose of *tikun olam* (societal remedy), we do not redeem captives for more than their worth.

QUESTIONS FOR DISCUSSION

1. What does it mean "more than their worth"?

2. In what way does refusing to overpay for hostages accomplish *tikun olam*?

Text 10b

Talmud, Gitin 45a

הַאי מִפְּנֵי תִיקּוּן הָעוֹלָם מִשּׁוּם דּוֹחֲקָא דְצִבּוּרָא הוּא,

אוֹ דִילְמָא מִשּׁוּם דְּלָא לִגְרְבוּ וְלַיְיתוּ טְפֵי?

What is the *tikun olam?* Is the concern about a financial burden on the community? Or, perhaps, that overpaying will incentivize more kidnappings?

Babylonian Talmud

A literary work of monumental proportions that draws upon the legal, spiritual, intellectual, ethical, and historical traditions of Judaism. The 37 tractates of the Babylonian Talmud contain the teachings of the Jewish sages from the period after the destruction of the 2nd Temple through the 5th century CE. It has served as the primary vehicle for the transmission of the Oral Law and the education of Jews over the centuries; it is the entry point for all subsequent legal, ethical, and theological Jewish scholarship.

Text 10c

ibid.

תָּא שְׁמַע: דְּלַוִי בַּר דַּרְגָּא פַּרְקָא לִבְרַתֵּיהּ בִּתְלֵיסַר אַלְפֵי דִּינָרֵי זְהַב.

Come and hear [a proof]: Levi bar Darga redeemed his daughter for thirteen thousand gold coins.

QUESTION FOR DISCUSSION

How might this incident prove whether the rationale for the ban was due to the communal financial burden or the future security risk?

Text 10d

Ibid. 📖

אמר אביי: ומאן לימא לן דברצון חכמים עבד, דילמא שלא ברצון חכמים עבד?

Abaye retorted: Why assume that Levi bar Darga acted in accordance with the wishes of the sages? Maybe he acted contrary to their wishes!

Text 11

Rabbi Yosef Caro, Shulchan Aruch, *Yoreh De'ah* 252:4 📖

אין פודין השבויים יותר מכדי דמיהם, מפני תיקון העולם,
שלא יהיו האויבים מוסרים עצמם עליהם לשבותם.

We do not overpay when redeeming captives. This is for *tikun olam*—so that our enemies will not target us and attempt to take us captive.

QUESTION FOR DISCUSSION

Based on the sources we have thus far seen, would Jewish law support or forbid the paying of ransom or releasing terror suspects in exchange for the release of an innocent hostage?

Exceptional Circumstances

Text 12

Talmud, Gitin 58a 📖

מעשה ברבי יהושע בן חנניה שהלך לכרך גדול שברומי. אמרו לו תינוק אחד
יש בבית האסורים, יפה עינים, וטוב רואי, וקווצותיו סדורות לו תלתלים.

הלך ועמד על פתח בית האסורים. אמר: "מי נתן למשיסה יעקב
וישראל לבוזזים" (ישעיהו מב,כד)? ענה אותו תינוק ואמר: "הלא ה'
זו חטאנו לו ולא אבו בדרכיו הלוך ולא שמעו בתורתו" (שם).

אמר: מובטחני בו שמורה הוראה בישראל. העבודה שאיני
זז מכאן עד שאפדנו בכל ממון שפוסקין עליו.

אמרו: לא זז משם עד שפדאו בממון הרבה. ולא היו ימים מועטין
עד שהורה הוראה בישראל. ומנו רבי ישמעאל בן אלישע.

Rabbi Yehoshua ben Chanania went to Rome. They told him: There is a [Jewish] child in prison, with beautiful eyes, attractive features, and pretty curls.

Rabbi Yehoshua went and stood at the entrance to the prison. He recited the first half of Isaiah 42:24: "Who subjected Jacob to plunder and Israel to spoilers?" The boy responded [with the second half of the verse]: "Was it not God? That we sinned against Him, and they did not want to go in His way, and did not hearken to His Torah."

Rabbi Yehoshua said, "I am sure this child will be a teacher of Israel. I will not move from this place until I redeem him for all the money they ask."

It was said that he didn't move from there until he redeemed the child for a large sum of money. And it wasn't long before the boy became a teacher in Israel. And who was this child? Rabbi Yishmael ben Elisha.

Text 13

Tosafot, ad loc. 📖

כי איכא סכנת נפשות, פודין שבויין יותר על כדי דמיהן.

When [the captive's] life is in danger, we may redeem him for more than his worth.

Tosafot

A collection of French and German Talmudic commentaries written during the 12th and 13th centuries. Among the most famous authors of *Tosafot* are Rabbi Ya'akov Tam, Rabbi Shimshon ben Avraham of Sens, and Rabbi Yitschak ("the Ri"). Printed in almost all editions of the Talmud, these commentaries are fundamental to basic Talmudic study.

Text 14

Talmud, Bava Batra 8b

אמר ליה רבא לרבה בר מרי: מנא הא מילתא דאמור

רבנן ד"פדיון שבוים מצוה רבה היא"?

אמר ליה: דכתיב (ירמיהו טו,ב) "והיה כי יאמרו אליך אנה נצא, ואמרת אליהם,

כה אמר ה', אשר למות למות, ואשר לחרב לחרב, ואשר לרעב לרעב ,ואשר

לשבי לשבי". ואמר רבי יוחנן: כל המאוחר בפסוק זה קשה מחבירו. חרב קשה

ממות . . . רעב קשה מחרב . . . שבי קשה מכולם, דכולהו איתנהו ביה.

Said Rava to Raba bar Mari: What is the source of the sages' assertion that redeeming captives is "a great mitzvah"?

Said Raba: For it says (Jeremiah 15:2), "And if [the Jewish people] ask you, 'Where shall we go?' tell them, 'This is what God says: "Those destined for death, to death; those for the sword, to the sword; those for starvation, to starvation; those for captivity, to captivity."'" Rabbi Yochanan said that there is a progression in this verse from bad to worse. Death by sword is worse than a natural death . . . death by hunger is worse than death by sword . . . and captivity is worse than all of them because it includes all of them.

QUESTION FOR DISCUSSION

In what way might this text contradict the position of *Tosafot*?

Text 15

Rabbi Moshe ben Nachman
(Nachmanides, Ramban)
1194–1270

Scholar, philosopher, author and physician. Nachmanides was born in Spain and served as leader of Iberian Jewry. In 1263, he was summoned by King James of Aragon to a public disputation with Pablo Cristiani, a Jewish apostate. Though Nachmanides was the clear victor of the debate, he had to flee Spain because of the resulting persecution. He moved to Israel and helped reestablish communal life in Jerusalem. He authored a classic commentary on the Pentateuch and a commentary on the Talmud.

Ramban, Gitin 45a 📖

ויש אומרים דכל היכא דאיכא חששא דמיתה,

פודין אותן בכל ממון שיכולין לפדותן.

ולא מסתבר, דכל שבי כולהו איתנהו ביה.

There are those who say that we overpay to redeem a captive whenever there is a concern for his life.

This, however, does not seem to be true because [the Talmud implies that] every captive is in danger.

QUESTION FOR DISCUSSION

How might have *Tosafot* responded to this objection?

Based on Texts 12–15, would Jewish law support or forbid the paying of ransom or releasing terror suspects in exchange for the release of an innocent hostage?

Why the Modern Reality Might Differ

Text 16

Rabbi Yehudah Gershuni, *Kol Tsofecha*, pp. 239–240

דבמקום סכנת נפשות פודין את השבויים יותר מכדי דמיהם . . .

והנה המצב בארץ ישראל לגמרי שונה. שהמחבלים הרוצחים שהעמידו
למטרתם לרצוח יהודים ומחזיקים יהודים שתפסו לשחרר על ידם סכום גדול
של מחבלים תחת כמה שבויים יהודים. והמחבלים הערבים כשיוציאו אותם
לחופש יתארגנו מחדש לרצוח יהודים ולסדר מעשה חבלה בכל גבולי הארץ
ואפילו בפנים בארץ ישראל. הרי יש סכנת נפשות נגד סכנת נפשות, סכנת
נפשות של השבויים נגד סכנת נפשות של אנשי הישוב, שעל ידי שחרור
המחבלים יתרבו מעשה רציחה על ישובים עבריים. וכי דוחין נפש מפני נפש?

When the captive is in mortal danger, we may overpay for his release. . . .

However, the situation in Israel is completely different. The terrorists have established a goal of murdering Jews. They hold a few Jews captive in order to gain the release of many terrorists. The freed terrorists will regroup and organize to murder Jews and to commit acts of terror

Rabbi Yehudah Gershuni
1912–2000

Born in Grodna, he studied in Kamenetz under Rabbi Baruch Ber Lebovitz. In 1933, he immigrated to Israel and lectured at Yeshivat Mercaz HaRav. He later lived in the United States and headed a yeshivah there, only to return to Israel in 1974 where he became one of editors of the *Talmudic Encyclopedia*.

throughout the Land. Thus, we are faced with conflicting cases of mortal danger: the mortal danger of the current captives versus the mortal danger of all dwellers of the Land once the terrorists are released and commit murderous acts on Jewish communities. Do we surrender one life in order to save another?

Text 17

Rabbi Shne'ur Zalman of Liadi, *Shulchan Aruch HaRav*, *Orach Chayim* 329:8 ▪

מצוה על כל אדם לחלל עליהם שבת כדי להצילם. ואפילו הוא ספק אם יציל.

ומכל מקום אם יש סכנה, אין לו לסכן עצמו כדי להציל את חבירו מאחר שהוא חוץ מן הסכנה. ואף שרואה במיתת חבירו, ואף על פי שהוא ספק וחבירו ודאי, מכל מקום הרי נאמר "וחי בהם" (ויקרא יח,ה) ולא שיבא לידי ספק מיתה על ידי שיקיים מה שנאמר "לא תעמוד על דם רעך" (ויקרא יט,טז).

Rabbi Shne'ur Zalman of Liadi
(Alter Rebbe)
1745–1812

Chasidic rebbe, halachic authority, and founder of the Chabad movement. The Alter Rebbe was born in Liozna, Belarus, and was among the principal students of the Magid of Mezeritch. His numerous works include the *Tanya*, an early classic containing the fundamentals of Chabad Chasidism, and *Shulchan Aruch HaRav*, an expanded and reworked code of Jewish law.

It is a mitzvah for each of us to desecrate the Shabbat in order to rescue others [whose lives are in danger]. This applies even if it is doubtful whether the rescue attempt will be successful.

Nevertheless, a person who is not in danger should not risk his life in order to save another. The law is such even if this means that the bystander will witness the death of another, and despite the fact that an attempt to rescue is only a possible danger for the rescuer whereas the victim is in certain danger. The Torah states, "And you shall live by them" (Leviticus 18:5), which implies that one should not risk possible death by fulfilling the mitzvah of "You shall not stand by the shedding of your fellow's blood" (Leviticus 19:16).

A Soldier—Different?

Text 18

Rabbi Chaim David Halevi, *Responsa Aseh Lecha Rav* 7:53 📖

כפי שהוברר בין היתר על ידי שר הבטחון, נגד עיני הממשלה שהחליטה, עמדה נקודה חשובה נוספת והיא המורל של חיילי צה"ל. כאשר חייל יודע שאם יפול בשבי, מדינת ישראל כולה ניצבת מאחריו לשחררו, ימסור נפשו בשעת קרב ללא פחד ומורא. אך אם יופעל הדין שאין פודין שבויים יתר על כדי דמיהן, גם במקרה זה, כאשר חיילים נשלחים בשליחות האומה למלחמה, אז מן הסתם יאמר כל חייל בלבו מוטב לסגת ולא ליפול בשבי. ומי הוא זה אשר ימדוד עתה מה הנזק הביטחוני הגדול יותר, חיזוק כוחם של המחבלים על ידי שחרור חבריהם, או חיזוק המורל של חיילי צה"ל במלחמות עתידות אם תקראנה ח"ו . . .

לכן, אין נראה לפי עניות דעתי שממשלת ישראל פעלה בניגוד להלכה . . . ועל כל פנים, לאחר מעשה ודאי שאין להרהר ואין לערער אחרי החלטת ממשלת ישראל על החלטתה. אף כי יש מקום לדון ולקבוע דרכי פעולה בעתיד לכל מקרה ח"ו.

The Minister of Defense (amongst others) clarified: Confronting the government that made this decision was an important additional point: the morale of the IDF's soldiers. When a soldier knows that were he to fall captive, the whole State of Israel stands behind him

Rabbi Hayim David Halevi
1924–1998

Sephardic chief rabbi of Tel Aviv-Jaffa. Rabbi Halevi was born in Jerusalem and studied under Rabbi Ben-Zion Meir Hai Uziel. When the latter was appointed Sephardic chief rabbi of Israel, he hired Rabbi Halevi as his personal secretary. In 1997, Halevi was awarded the Israel Prize for his contributions in the field of Judaic studies.

to set him free, he will commit himself entirely to battle without fear. However, if the rule that prisoners will not be ransomed for an excessive price is applied to soldiers, then when they are sent out on their missions, we may assume that they will think in their hearts, "Better for me to retreat and not to fall prisoner." Who now can measure which is greater: strengthening the terrorists by releasing their comrades, or strengthening the morale of the IDF soldiers in any future wars that might happen, God forbid? . . .

Therefore, in my humble opinion, it does not seem that the government of Israel has acted against Halachah. . . . At the least, it is certain that one must not second-guess or delegitimize the government's decision after it has been made, even though there is still place to deliberate and to decide on paths of action in any future event, God forbid.

Text 19

Rabbi Shlomo Goren, *Torat Hamedinah*, p. 436

אולם על אף האמור לעיל, יתכן שבמקרה של שבויי מלחמה של חיילים שנשבו תוך מילוי שליחותם של המדינה ששלחה אותם למשימות של מלחמה, מוטלת חובה קדושה לעשות הכל כדי לשחררם, ואין עליהם כלל את המגבלות של המשנה "אין פודים את השבויים יתר על כדי דמיהם", משום שחיילנו נפלו בשבי במילוי שליחות המדינה. ייתכן ועל המדינה מוטלת החובה הבלתי מעורערת לפדותם ולהוציא אותם מהסכנה הקלה ביותר, ואין עליהם שום מגבלות של פדיון שבויים דעלמא. משום שהמדינה חייבת לפדותם בכל ממון שבעולם ובכל מחיר שהוא, משום שהאחריות על חייהם מוטלת על המדינה ששלחה אותם לקרב ממנו לא חזרו. ואין להתחשב בעת שחרורם בסיכון בטחוני כביכול שישחרורם עלול לגרום לציבור ולמדינה, מפני שכל שאנו אחראים לנפילתם בשבי, עלינו לעשות כל מאמץ לשחרר אותם מהשבי ואפילו שלא נשקפת להם סכנה בשבי.

Despite what I stated earlier, it is possible that in the case of prisoners of war who were captured while fulfilling the mission of the country that tasked them with battle, that there is a sacred obligation to do all that is possible to free them, without any constrains by the ruling that we may not overpay for redeeming captives. The soldiers fell captive while fulfilling the mission of the country. It is possible, therefore, that the country has an incontestable obligation to ransom them, using any source of money and at any price, for the state that sent them to the battle from which they did not return bears the responsibility for their lives. We must not calculate the damage to security that their freeing is liable to cause to the public and the state. When we are responsible for their falling into captivity, we must make every effort to free them, even if there doesn't seem to be any likely danger to them as prisoners.

Rabbi Shlomo Goren
1917 –1994

Ashkenazic chief rabbi of Israel. Rabbi Goren was born in Poland and moved with his family to pre-state Israel in 1925. As a soldier in the 1948 war, Goren was often asked to help resolve specific questions concerning religious observance under wartime conditions. In 1948, he was named chief chaplain of the new state's army. He led the troops who liberated the Western Wall during the Six-Day War in prayer and blew a *shofar* to mark the occasion. In 1972, he was elected Israel's chief Ashkenazic rabbi and served until 1983.

ISRAEL: LEGAL ASPECTS OF PRISONER EXCHANGES

RUTH LEVUSH

Summary

Israel has engaged in prisoner-swap deals numerous times throughout its history. The release of members of organizations it considers to be terrorist organizations and of those convicted of terrorism-related offenses has been increasingly contested by the Israeli public.

Members of victims' families and victims' organizations have petitioned the Supreme Court to impose limits on presidential and governmental discretion to approve prisoner releases. In response to claims made by petitioners the Court has established requirements for mandatory prior notice and disclosure of the names of prisoners whose release is being considered. The Court has also recognized the procedures that must be followed to enable members of victims' families to object to the release of the killers of their loved ones. The Court, however, refrained from reviewing the merits of governmental decisions to release prisoners or to determine that they were adopted without legal authority and refused to order the government to adopt any fixed rules that would determine principles for future negotiations.

In 2010 a committee was appointed by the Minister of Defense to review Israel's past practices of prisoner releases and determine principles for conducting negotiations for the release of captives. The committee's report was presented to the Israeli government in 2012. The report, however, remains classified, and the guidelines proposed by the committee have not been published.

A government bill to authorize judges to sentence persons who have committed murder for nationalistic motives to life without parole is currently being considered by the Knesset (Israel's Parliament). The Bill proposes to remove the authority of the President to grant clemency to persons who have been sentenced to life without parole, thereby making it impossible in the future to release convicted murderers under circumstances provided by law either as part of a prisoner-swap deal or as a gesture of good faith in negotiations with the Palestinian Authority. If adopted into law, this Bill would apply only to persons convicted of murder and not to those convicted of lesser offenses or to detainees held by the Israel Defense Forces.

I. Introduction

There is an ongoing public debate in Israel over the "cost" of releasing nationals held by groups considered by the country to be terrorist organizations. The debate over prisoner exchanges in Israel reflects a moral as well as religious dilemma. The rescue of those in captivity, known in Hebrew as *pidyon shevuyim*, has traditionally been considered a basic obligation under Jewish law and has been followed in Jewish communities for generations. The obligation to rescue captives under Jewish law is not, however, without limits.[1]

Israel has engaged in prisoner-swap deals with terrorist organizations numerous times during its history.[2] While the circumstances that have led to the capture of Israelis by terrorist organizations have varied, the cost involved in their release has steadily increased. The last release in 2011 involved the exchange of 1,027 Palestinian prisoners, including hundreds that had been convicted of murder-related offenses in Israeli courts, for the release of one Israeli soldier. The soldier, Gilad Shalit, had been abducted by the military wing of Hamas from inside Israel's

---

[1] *See Baruch S. Davidson, Is Prisoner Exchange A Jewish Value? Judaism's Take on Redeeming Prisoners*, CHABAD.ORG, http://www.chabad.org/library/article_cdo/aid/1668252/jewish/Is-Prisoner-Exchange-A-Jewish-Value.htm (last visited June 12, 2014).

[2] A partial list covering prisoners exchanges, from the hijacking of the 1968 El-Al and the 1969 TWA flights up to the kidnapping of two Israeli soldiers near the Lebanese border in 2006, is available in Ariel Gilboa, The Influence of "The Cost" in Negotiations for Release of Kidnapped [Persons] from Terrorist Organizations (Final Thesis for the Degree of Masters in Public Policy, The Hebrew University, Jan. 2010), http://public-policy.huji.ac.il/.upload/ Thesis_HE/Ariel_Gilboa_thesis.pdf (in Hebrew).

borders in June 2006 and held captive by Hamas for over five years.[3]

As with prisoner exchanges, many Israelis have contested the release of members of terrorist organizations as gestures of good will in the course of negotiations with the Palestinian Authority. Since August 2013 Israel has released seventy-eight Palestinians "in three batches as part of a framework deal that led to eight months of negotiations with the Palestinian Liberation Organization (PLO). Israel refused to release a final batch of 26 terrorists when it appeared the talks would not be extended past their nine-month deadline."[4]

The appropriateness of releasing terrorists in exchange for Israelis held by terrorist organizations has been the focus of a review by a special committee appointed by the Minister of Defense. In addition, various aspects of prisoner releases have been reviewed by Israel's Supreme Court in response to petitions filed by members of families of victims and by victims' organizations.

Discontent with the mounting cost of prisoner exchanges has led to the introduction of a number of bills in the Knesset. These bills called for limiting the power of the President of the State to grant clemency and commute sentences of terrorists convicted of murder, as well as for generally restricting governmental discretion on the release of terrorists.[5]

This report analyzes the legal aspects of the release of terrorism detainees as well as of those convicted by Israeli courts of terrorism-related offenses. The report covers Israeli law as applicable at the time of its writing and will be updated as necessary.

II. Shamgar Committee on Determination of Principles for Conducting Negotiations for Release of Captives

In response to increasing concerns voiced by the Israeli public, in 2010 then-Israeli Minister of Defense Ehud Barak appointed Retired Supreme Court Justice Meir Shamgar to head the Committee on Determination of Principles for Conducting Negotiations for the Release of Captives. The Committee reviewed Israel's past prisoner exchanges and was tasked with proposing new principles for conducting negotiations for the release of Israeli captives in the future.

The Committee determined that its recommendations would not apply to the release of Gilad Shalit, who was in captivity at the time of its appointment. The Committee interviewed senior military officials after Shalit's release, however, and considered the lessons learned from the negotiations for his release before adopting its recommendations. According to Shamgar, the Committee deliberated not only on "how to conclude negotiations, but also on whether to conduct negotiations, and on what are the permitted boundaries and the [relevant] determining authorities."[6]

The Committee presented its report to the government in January 2012.[7] The first time the military cabinet reportedly conducted a hearing to discuss the Committee's recommendations, however, was two and a half years later, on June 5, 2014. The recommendations were discussed in connection with a bill promoted by the Bayit Yehudi political faction regarding prisoner releases.[8] Having been classified as "highly secretive," the Committee's report has not been disclosed to the Israeli public.

In a press conference held on January 5, 2012, subsequent to the issuing of the report, Committee Chair-

---

[3] *See* Ruth Levush, *Prisoner Swap Deals Under Israeli Law*, IN CUSTODIA LEGIS (Nov. 16, 2011), http://blogs.loc. gov/law/2011/11/prisoners-swap-deals-under-israeli-lawhats-the-worth-of-one-life-prisoner-swap-deals-under-israeli-law/.

[4] Herb Keinon & Lahav Harkov, *Cabinet Okays Bill Curbing Presidential Powers to Free Terrorists*, JERUSALEM POST (June 8, 2014), http://www.jpost.com/Diplomacy-and-Politics/Israel-okays-bill-that-would-limit-pardons-of-Palestinian-terrorists-355657.

[5] Information on proposed bills is available on the Knesset website at http://main.knesset.gov.il/Activity/ Legislation/Pages/default.aspx.

[6] Gili Cohen, *The Shamgar Committee: There Is a Need to Toughen Positions in Future Negotiations on Release of Captives*, HAARETZ (Jan. 6, 2012), http://www.haaretz.co.il/news/politics/1.1610579 (this and other translations from Hebrew in this report by author, R.L.).

[7] *Id.*

[8] Barak Ravid, *The Cabinet Will Discuss the Recommendations of the Shamgar Committee on Captives' Deals*, HAARETZ (June 5, 2014), http://www.haaretz.co.il/news/politics/.premium-1.2340159 (in Hebrew); for information regarding the proposed legislation *see* part III of this report.

man Shamgar disclosed that the Committee had recommended the transfer of responsibility from the Prime Minister's Office to the Ministry of Defense for both negotiating on prisoner releases and maintaining contact with captives' families. The Committee had further recommended that prisoner-swap deals in the future would be brought to the government for approval only after reaching an understanding with the "kidnapping" side.[9]

Reacting to the Committee's recommendations, Minister Barak commented at the time that it was important to stop the slippery slope on which we have gradually found ourselves since the first Gibril deal, through the second Gibril deal and Tenenbaum and up to Gilad himself. . . . [I]n the area where we live, a state that cherishes life will not be able to act efficiently and ensure in the long run the general interests of all [its] citizens if we do not change the rules, the reality, or the results as they were in the swap deals in the last 25 years.[10]

III. Proposed Legislation on Limiting Presidential and Executive Authority for Prisoner Releases

On June 11, 2014, the Knesset preliminarily approved Basic Law: President of the State (Amendment – Prohibition on Release of Murderers) Bill.[11] This Bill is the latest of several bills that have been introduced by Knesset members in recent years to limit presidential and executive powers to engage in the release of prisoners in exchange for Israeli nationals or as a gesture of good will in negotiations.[12]

The Bill had been submitted by the Bayit Yehudi faction Chairwoman Ayelet Shaked and additional Knesset members following the prisoner releases in the latest round of talks with the Palestinians.[13] The Bill proposes to limit presidential powers to grant clemency or commute life sentences of convicted murderers.[14]

Specifically, the Bill proposed to empower any court that sentences a person convicted of murder under section 300 of the Penal Law, 5737-1997 to a life sentence to "determine, for special reasons to be registered, that the President of the State will not grant [the convicted person] clemency and will not lessen his/her sentence. . . ."[15] Under section 300 of the Penal Law, a life sentence must be imposed on a person who has been convicted of the premeditated causation of the death of another.[16]

According to explanatory notes of the bill,

Israel has released a great number of terrorists as part of transactions for release of captives or as political gestures. The reality led to the absurd situation in which terrorists that committed murderous actions as part of their fight against the State of Israel are released a long time before completing their sentence. This fact constitutes a moral failure that [reflects] a devaluation of the severity of actions committed by terrorists and of the authority of the legal system in Israel. Additionally, currently the sentence of murderers [can be] commuted even if they conducted murders that are excessive in their severity, like murder of children.

This bill is intended to correct this state of affairs and prevent a situation where because of pressures . . . it will be decided to grant clemency as part of prisoner exchanges or as political gestures to terrorists that conducted murders.[17]

---

[9] Amir Buchbut, *Shamgar: "To Revoke the Subject of Captives from the Prime Minister,"* WALLA NEWS (Jan. 5, 2012), http://news.walla.co.il/?w=/9/1891423 (in Hebrew).

[10] Cohen, *supra* note 5.

[11] Basic Law: President of the State (Amendment – Prohibition on Release of Murderers) Bill No. 2113/19, http://www.knesset.gov.il/privatelaw/data/19/2113.rtf.

[12] *See, e.g.,* Release of Hostages and Kidnapped, Private Member Bill No. 2437/19, https://www.knesset.gov.il/ privatelaw/data/19/2437.rtf.

[13] Lahav Harkov, *Bayit Yehudi Furious as Netanyahu Delays Vote on Limiting Prisoner Releases,* JERUSALEM POST (June 1, 2014), http://

www.jpost.com/Diplomacy-and-Politics/Bayit-Yehudi-furious-as-Netanyahu-delays-vote-on-limiting-prisoner-releases-355020.

[14] Basic Law: President of the State (Amendment – Prohibition on Release of Murderers) Bill No. 2113/19

[15] *Id.*

[16] Penal Law 5737-1997, LAWS OF THE STATE OF ISRAEL (Special Volume).

[17] Basic Law: President of the State (Amendment – Prohibition on Release of Murderers) Bill No. 2113/19.

Prime Minister Binyamin Netanyahu had initially prevented a vote on the Bill in a government meeting on June 1, 2014, in consideration of a legal opinion issued by the Government Legal Adviser, Yehuda Weinstein. The opinion found a discrepancy between the Bill's explanatory notes, which focused on the intent to prevent the release of terrorists who had been convicted of murder, and the Bill's proposed language, which was more general and applied to other convicted murderers.[18] Weinstein has also reportedly expressed dismay that the government would want to pass a law that would restrict its discretion for many years to come.[19]

On June 7, 2014, however, the Israeli government approved a decision to promote the Bill on the basis of the report's recommendations and resolve the discrepancy between the text of the law and its explanatory notes.[20] The amended text has been preliminarily approved by the Knesset plenum. According to a Knesset press release on June 11, 2014, the Bill proposed that

> when special reasons exist, the court will be authorized to sentence a person who has been convicted of murder for nationalistic motives to a full penalty of life imprisonment without the possibility for commuting the penalty or receiving clemency from the President of the State [life without parole]. In addition, the bill is also intended to enable the court to determine that in murder cases that are especially heinous, such as in the murder of children, there will not be a possibility of commuting the penalty and clemency for the murderer.[21]

In accordance with Knesset rules, following its passage in the preliminary hearing, the Bill has been transferred to a Knesset committee for preparation for the second and third readings. The Bill will be adopted into law only after a majority vote in both readings. [22]

IV. Judicial Review of Prisoner Releases

Family members of terrorism victims and victims' organizations have contested the release of terrorists, especially those involved in the killing of their loved ones. The following is a summary of the most recent decisions rendered by the Supreme Court in petitions filed by victims' families and organizations.

A. HCJ 8646/13 Schijveschuurder v. State of Israel

The latest decision by the Supreme Court on this issue was rendered on December 26, 2013.[23] The petitioners lost five members of their family in the terrorist bombing on August 9, 2001, at the Sbarro restaurant in Jerusalem.[24]

Among other things, the petitioners requested the Court to determine that granting clemency to convicted prisoners, including two of the perpetrators of the bombing whose release they objected to, could only be made in accordance with Basic Law: The President of the State[25] and with Victims of Crime Rights Law 5761-2001.[26] They also argued that any release of convicted terrorists must be made in accordance with clear criteria that have been properly adopted. The petitioners further requested the disclosure of the Shamgar Committee's report on Deter-

---

[18] Yonatan Lis & Revital Hovel, *Netanyahu Prevented a Vote on a Law to Prohibit Release of Terrorists*, HAARETZ (June 1, 2014), http://www.haaretz.co.il/news/politics/1.2337403 (in Hebrew).

[19] *Id.*

[20] Yonatan Lis, *At the End of a Hotly Debated Hearing: The Government Approved the Law that Would Prevent Clemency for Terrorists*, HAARETZ (June 8, 2014), http://www.haaretz.co.il/news/politi/1.2342472#.U5Sggm-wjgc.email (in Hebrew).

[21] Press Release, Knesset, Approved in Preliminary [Plenum Vote]: Clemency for Murderers Will Not Be Possible (June 11, 2014), http://main.knesset.gov.il/News/PressReleases/Pages/press110614-aq.aspx (in Hebrew).

[22] *See The Knesset Work: Legislation*, KNESSET, http://knesset.gov.il/description/eng/eng_work_mel2.htm (last visited June 10, 2014).

[23] HCJ 8646/13 Schijveschuurder v. State of Israel [Dec. 26, 2013], http://elyon1.court.gov.il/files/13/460/086/c03/ 13086460.c03.pdf (this and all other cited court decisions are in Hebrew).

[24] For information, see Suzanne Goldenberg, *'The street was covered with blood and bodies: the dead and the dying'*, THE GUARDIAN (Aug. 9, 2001), http://www.theguardian.com/world/2001/aug/10/israel1; see also Omri Efraim, *Decade later, Sbarro attack still haunts victims*, YNETNEWS (Oct. 8, 2011), http://www.ynetnews.com/articles/0,7340,L-4106884,00.html

[25] Basic Law: The President of the State § 11(B), SEFER HAHUK-KIM [SH] No. 428, p. 118 (5724–1964), English translation *available at* http://knesset.gov.il/laws/special/eng/basic12_eng.htm.

[26] Victims of Crime Rights Law 5761-2001, SH No. 1782, p. 183, *as amended* (in Hebrew).

mination of Principles for Conducting Negotiations for the Release of Captives.[27]

Expressing sympathy with the petitioners' pain, Justice Miriam Naor nevertheless rejected the petition. She held that the issues raised by the petitioners in this petition had already been addressed in two earlier decisions, HCJ 5413/13 Almagor v. State of Israel, [28] and HCJ 5606/13 Schijveschuurder v. State of Israel. [29]

B. HCJ 5413/13 Almagor v. State of Israel

On August 11, 2013, the Israeli High Court of Justice rejected a petition by Almagor, the Association of Victims of Terrorism, and by members of victims' families to void a governmental decision to release Palestinian prisoners convicted of terrorism offenses as a good-will gesture during the course of renewed peace negotiations between Israel and the Palestinians.[30]

The subject of the petition is Government Decision No. 640, which was adopted by the Israeli government on July 28, 2013.[31] This decision authorized the government to convene a ministerial team that would determine the conditions, timing, and criteria for selecting prisoners to be released during peace negotiations, but required the names of those selected to be publically published.[32]

The Court rejected the petitioners' claims regarding the ministerial committee's alleged lack of jurisdiction and noncompliance with notice requirements. Court President Asher Grunis, with Justices Elyakim Rubinstein and Zvi Zilbertal concurring, held that the government was authorized to adopt a de-

cision on entering into political negotiations and on the release of prisoners, and that there was no need for an explicit authorization to this effect in primary legislation.

This conclusion, according to Grunis, was based on two earlier decisions by the High Court.[33] Unlike a declaration of war, he held, for which a decision of the full government is mandated by Basic Law: The Government,[34] a decision to release prisoners or enter into political negotiations does not require a full quorum under any law.[35]

Grunis also rejected the petitioners' claim that their rights under the Victims of Crime Rights Law 5761-2001[36] had been violated because they had not been afforded the opportunity to express their objections in writing. He reiterated the previously established principle that rights under this Law are not fully applicable to cases where clemency is not obtained through "a regular" criminal process but rather through a political agreement.[37]

Considering the tight time frame applicable under the circumstances, and the state's willingness to follow the established practice of allowing victims to express objections within forty-eight hours prior to the release of prisoners, Grunis refused to require that the state permit victims to object in writing under the procedures established by the Law. He also concluded that there was no need to extend the period available for objections beyond the forty-eight hours period offered by the state.[38]

---

[27] HCJ 8646/13 Schijveschuurder v. State of Israel.

[28] HCJ 5413/13 Almagor v. Government of Israel, http://elyon1.court.gov.il/files/13/130/054/s04/13054130.s04.pdf.

[29] HCJ 5606/13 Schijveschuurder v. State of Israel, http://elyon1.court.gov.il/files/13/060/056/l01/13056060.l01.pdf.

[30] HCJ 5413/13 Almagor v. Government of Israel.

[31] Approval of Opening of Political Negotiations Between Israel and the Palestinians in Accordance with the Prime Minister's Announcement Regarding the Negotiations and Authorization of the Ministerial Team for the Release of Palestinian Prisoners in the Course of the Negotiations, Government Decision No. 640 of July 28, 2013, http://www. pmo.gov.il/Secretary/GovDecisions/2013/Pages/des640.aspx (in Hebrew).

[32] Id.

[33] HCJ 5413/13 Almagor v. Government of Israel, para. 6 (referring to HCJ 1539/05 & 5272/05 Institute for Research of Terrorism and Assistance for its Victims v. the Prime Minister, http://elyon1.court.gov.il/verdictssearch/ HebrewVerdictsSearch.aspx, and http://elyon1.court.gov.il/verdictssearch/HebrewVerdictsSearch.aspx, respectively (both in Hebrew)).

[34] Basic Law: The Government (2001) § 40(a), http://knesset.gov.il/laws/special/eng/basic14_eng.htm.

[35] HCJ 5413/13 Almagor v. Government of Israel, para. 6.

[36] Victims of Crime Rights Law 5761-2001, SH No. 1782, p. 183, as amended.

[37] Id. para 7 (referring to HCJ 7523/11 Almagor – Organization of Victims of Terrorism v. the Prime Minister, http://elyon1.court.gov.il/files/11/230/075/n05/11075230.n05.pdf (in Hebrew)). For information on the Almagor decision, see Levush, supra note 3.

[38] Victims of Crime Rights Law 5761-2001, SH No. 1782 p. 183, as amended.

Further rejecting the petitioners' claims, Justice Grunis determined that decisions regarding the release of prisoners, especially those adopted in the course of political negotiations, are within the authority and discretion of the government based on its responsibility to further the state's foreign relations and ensure public security.[39]

Considering the circumstances that existed in that case, the Court rejected the claim that the decision to release the prisoners by the method determined in the government decision was affected by an extreme lack of reasonableness. The Court also rejected the claim that the government decision in this regard suffered from any other defect that required judicial intervention.[40]

C. HCJ 5606/13 Schijveschuurder v. State of Israel

On August 13, 2013, two days after rendering the decision in HCJ 5413/13 Almagor v. State of Israel, the Supreme Court rejected a petition by members of the Schijveschuurder family,[41] the same petitioners in the previously discussed decision in HCJ 8646/13 Schijveschuurder v. State of Israel. The Court reiterated that it would refrain from intervening in decisions to release prisoners either as part of prisoner-swap deals or as an expression of good will in negotiations because of the political nature of such decisions.[42]

The Court further rejected the petitioners' claims that the planned prisoners' release to which they objected violated the clemency authorities of the President. According to the Court, the procedures that applied to the prisoners' release in this case complied with the requirements established in the earlier case of HCJ 9446/09 Karman v. Prime Minister of Israel.[43] According to these requirements the petitioners as well as other bereaved families had a right to obtain information on prisoners that might be released and

to direct their objections to their release to the clemency department of the Ministry of Justice. Their objections must also be forwarded to the President of the State.[44]

The Court rejected the petitioners' request to require the adoption of fixed criteria for prisoner releases. Justice Tzvi Zilberstein stated for the Court that "there is a difficulty in tying the discretion of the determining agency to harsh criteria when it is impossible to foresee in which future cases, and under which conditions it will have to adopt decisions on these difficult issues."[45]

V. Conclusion

The release of convicted violent terrorists or members of terrorist organizations in prisoner exchanges or as good-will gestures has been the subject of fierce public debate in Israel. Objections to prisoner releases have mounted in view of the constant rise in the cost associated with such transactions. Public disagreement was particularly vocal over the number of Palestinians released by Israel—1,027—in exchange for Gilad Shalit.

Arguments against the cost associated with prisoner exchanges have focused on their utility—namely, the increased motivation of terrorist organizations to kidnap Israeli soldiers to free their members, thereby affecting Israeli counterterrorism deterrence efforts. Strong objections were similarly expressed to "lessening the severity of terrorists' actions and the authority of the legal system in Israel,"[46] as a result of commuting the sentences of murderers, specifically those who committed murderous offenses that are extraordinary in their severity, such as the murder of children. In addition, many Israelis, particularly families of terrorism victims, have rallied against the release of these killers. They have demanded the adoption of transparent criteria and procedures for terrorists' release.

---

39 *Id.* para. 10.

40 *Id.*

41 HCJ 5606/13 Schijveschuurder v. State of Israel, http://elyon1.court.gov.il/files/13/060/056/l01/13056060.l01.pdf.

42 *Id.* ¶ 5.

43 HCJ 9446/09 Karman v. Prime Minister of Israel, http://elyon1.court.gov.il/files/09/460/094/n03/09094460 .n03.pdf.

44 HCJ 5606/13 Schijveschuurder v. State of Israel, ¶ 7.

45 *Id.* ¶ 8.

46 Press Release, Knesset, *supra* note 21.

In response to the mounting concerns associated with prisoner-swap deals, a committee was appointed to study Israel's experience in this area and to propose new principles for conducting negotiations for the release of Israeli captives in the future. The committee's report was issued in 2012 but has not been publically disclosed and remains classified. According to media reports, however, there is no doubt that among its recommendations was the introduction of a more conservative approach to Israel's future engagement in prisoner-swap deals and a limitation on the price that can be paid to obtain the freedom of captives.

The implementation of presidential authority to grant clemency and commute sentences, and of governmental compliance with procedural requirements involving prisoner releases, has been repeatedly reviewed by the Supreme Court. The Court has established specific requirements with regard to providing notice to victims' families, disclosing the names of prisoners considered for release, and providing opportunities to object to the release. The Court refused, however, to order the government to adopt criteria that would limit governmental discretion in the future. It has similarly refused to order a public disclosure of the Shamgar Committee report and its recommendations.

In the absence of a judicial restriction on prisoner releases, opponents of prisoner releases have called for restricting governmental and presidential authority in this area by legislation. Currently, a government bill is being prepared for second and third readings before the Knesset plenum. This bill, however, is limited in scope and appears to apply only to the release of persons convicted of murder.

If passed, the bill will not affect the government's future discretion to engage in the release of persons convicted of offenses less serious than murder, nor will it affect government discretion to release persons detained by military authorities who have not been convicted by Israeli courts. Although not subject to the restrictions established by the bill, governmental discretion in these cases is not unlimited. As discussed above, the government must comply with the requirements for notice and consideration of victims' families' objections that were established by the Supreme Court. In addition, the government will also be guided by the recommendations of the Shamgar Committee, recommendations that so far have not been publically disclosed.

The legal developments in this area reflect uncertainty as to whether Israel will engage in prisoner-swap deals of the type conducted in the Shalit case in the future. If the latest government bill on restricting clemency and commuting life sentences for convicted murderers passes, persons convicted of murder for nationalistic motives will not be released in future prisoner-swap deals. With regard to other prisoners, from the little that was made public about the Shamgar Committee's recommendations, it appears that "Israel will release only a few security prisoners and not tens or thousands . . . in return for one Israeli captive, in order to prevent [future] mega deals for prisoner exchanges."[47]

The Law Library of Congress, Global Legal Research Center,
June 2014
http://www.loc.gov

47 Gili Cohen, *The Shamgar Committee: There Is a Need to Toughen Positions in Future Negotiations on Release of Captives*, HAARETZ (Jan. 6, 2012), http://www.haaretz.co.il/news/politics/1.1610579 (translated from Hebrew by R.L.).

JUSTICE AND THE WAR ON TERROR

LESSON 2

The Ticking-Bomb Dilemma

The recently released "Torture Report" alleges that the harsh interrogative methods used by the C.I.A. in the aftermath of 9/11 were ineffective. Others argue that the report cherry-picked information to support the claim that the program yielded no valuable information.

But even if the program did yield valuable information, would it have been justified? While the evils of terror must be combated, human rights must also be protected. How are we to balance these competing values?

JLI

JEWISH LEARNING INSTITUTE

Case Studies

Text 1

Kathryn Sikkink, *The Justice Cascade: How Human Rights Prosecutions Are Changing World Politics* [New York: W.W. Norton & Co., 2011], p. 214

Ernesto Sabato, the writer who was the chair of the Argentine Commission, wrote in the prologue to the commission's report *Nunca Mas* of the Italian government's struggle against violent groups like the Red Brigades: "Never at any time, however, did that country abandon the principles of law in its fight against these terrorists.... When [former Prime Minister] Aldo Moro was kidnapped, a member of the security forces suggested to General Della Chiesa that a suspect who apparently knew a lot be tortured. The General replied with the memorable words: 'Italy can survive the loss of Aldo Moro. It would not survive the introduction of torture.'"

QUESTION FOR DISCUSSION

Do you agree with General Della Chiesa's decision? Explain your reasoning.

Text 2

Leon v. State, 410 So. 2d 201 (Fla. Dist. Ct. App. 1982)

For the very good reason that Louis's life was in grave danger from Armand if Leon (or the officers) did not return within a short time, the police immediately demanded that the defendant tell them where he was. When he at first refused, he was set upon by several of the officers. They threatened and physically abused him by twisting his arm behind his back and choking him until he revealed where Louis was being held. The officers went to the designated apartment, rescued Louis and arrested Armand.

QUESTIONS FOR DISCUSSION

1. Do you agree with the officers' decision to physically coerce Jean Leon to reveal the whereabouts of Louis Gachelin?

2. Are there material differences between this case and the case of Aldo Moro? What are they?

Text 3

Matthew Brzezinski, "Bust and Boom," *Washington Post*, December 30, 2001

Philippine intelligence put the screws to Murad. In Camp Crame, a military installation on the outskirts of Manila, he was subjected for 67 days to what Philippine intelligence reports delicately refer to as TI, or tactical interrogation. By the time he was handed over to the Americans, interrogators had extracted everything they thought they needed to know.

QUESTIONS FOR DISCUSSION

1. Under these circumstances, was the "tactical interrogation" the right thing to do?

2. Are there material differences between this case and the previous cases? What are they?

Text 4

John H. Langbein, *Torture and the Law of Proof: Europe and England in the Ancien Régime* [Chicago, University of Chicago Press, 1977], p. 4

The Roman-canon law of proof governed judicial procedure in cases of serious crime, cases where blood sanctions (death or severe physical maiming) could be imposed. In brief, there were three fundamental rules.

First, the court could convict and condemn an accused upon the testimony of two eyewitnesses to the gravamen of the crime.

Second, if there were not two eyewitnesses, the court could convict and condemn the accused only upon the basis of his own confession.

Third, circumstantial evidence, so called *indicia*, was not an adequate basis for conviction and condemnation, no matter how compelling. It does not matter, for example, that the suspect is seen running away from the murdered man's house and that the bloody dagger and the stolen loot are found in his possession. The court cannot convict him of the crime.

At least, the court cannot convict him without his confession, and that is where torture fitted into the system. In certain cases where there was neither the voluntary confession nor the testimony of the two eyewitnesses, the court could order that the suspect be examined about the crime under torture in order to secure his confession.

Text 5

Michael Walzer, "Political Action: The Problem of Dirty Hands,"
Philosophy and Public Affairs 2 (1973), pp. 166–167

Consider a politician who has seized upon a national crisis—a prolonged colonial war—to reach for power. He and his friends win office pledged to decolonization and peace. . . . Immediately, the politician goes off to the colonial capital to open negotiations with the rebels. But the capital is in the grip of a terrorist campaign, and the first decision the new leader faces is this: he is asked to authorize the torture of a captured rebel leader who knows or probably knows the location of a number of bombs hidden in apartment buildings around the city, set to go off within the next twenty-four hours. He orders the man tortured, convinced that he must do so for the sake of the people who might otherwise die in the explosions—even though he believes that torture is wrong, indeed abominable, not just sometimes, but always. He had expressed this belief often and angrily during his own campaign; the rest of us took it as a sign of his goodness. How should we regard him now? (How should he regard himself?)

QUESTIONS FOR DISCUSSION

1. Did the politician make the more ethical choice?

2. Are there material differences between this case and the previous cases? What are they?

Law of the Land

Text 6

Alan Dershowitz, *Why Terrorism Works*
[New Haven, CT: Yale University Press, 2002], p. 135

The Fifth Amendment prohibits compelled self-incrimination, which means that statements elicited by means of torture may not be introduced into evidence against the defendant who has been tortured. But if a suspect is given immunity and then tortured into providing information about a future terrorist act, his privilege against self-incrimination has not been violated. . . . Nor has his right to be free from "cruel and unusual punishment," since the provision of the Eighth Amendment has been interpreted to apply solely to punishment after conviction.

Text 7

Leon v. Wainwright, 734 F. 2d 770 (11th Cir. 1984)

Unlike most cases involving coercion to obtain confessions, the police's motive in this case was totally different. The violence was not inflicted to obtain a confession or provide other evidence to establish appellant's guilt. Instead it was motivated by the immediate necessity to find the victim and save his life.

Text 8

Ingraham v. Wright, 430 U.S. 651 (1977)

The Eighth Amendment provides: "Excessive bail shall not be required, nor excessive fines imposed, nor cruel and unusual punishments inflicted." Bail, fines, and punishment traditionally have been associated with the criminal process, and by subjecting the three to parallel limitations the text of the Amendment suggests an intention to limit the power of those entrusted with the criminal-law function of government. An examination of the history of the Amendment and the decisions of this Court construing the proscription against cruel and unusual punishment confirms that it was designed to protect those convicted of crimes. We adhere to this long-standing limitation and hold that the Eighth Amendment does not apply to the paddling of children as a means of maintaining discipline in public schools. . . .

In the few cases where the Court has had occasion to confront claims that impositions outside the criminal process constituted cruel and unusual punishment, it has had no difficulty finding the Eighth Amendment inapplicable. Thus, in *Fong Yue Ting v. United States*, 149 U.S. 698 (1893), the Court held the Eighth Amendment inapplicable to the deportation of aliens on the ground that "deportation is not a punishment for crime." Id., at 730; see *Mahler v. Eby*, 264 U.S. 32 (1924); *Bugajewitz v. Adams*, 228 U.S. 585 (1913). And in *Uphaus v. Wyman*, 360 U.S. 72 (1959), the Court sustained a judgment of civil contempt, resulting in incarceration pending compliance with a subpoena, against a claim that the judgment imposed cruel and unusual punishment. It was emphasized that the case involved "'essentially a civil remedy designed for the benefit of other parties . . . exercised for centuries to secure compliance with judicial decrees." Id., at 81, quoting *Green v. United States*, 356 U.S. 165, 197 (1958) (dissenting opinion).

Text 9a

United Nations Convention against Torture, Articles 1–2

For the purposes of this Convention, the term "torture" means any act by which severe pain or suffering, whether physical or mental, is intentionally inflicted on a person for such purposes as obtaining from him or a third person information or a confession, punishing him for an act he or a third person has committed or is suspected of having committed, or intimidating or coercing him or a third person, or for any reason based on discrimination of any kind, when such pain or suffering is inflicted by or at the instigation of or with the consent or acquiescence of a public official or other person acting in an official capacity. . . .

Text 9b

Alan Dershowitz, *Why Terrorism Works* [New Haven, CT: Yale University Press, 2002], p. 135

The United States adopted the convention, but with a reservation: we agreed to be bound by it "only to the extent that it is consistent with . . . the Eighth Amendment." Decisions by U.S. courts have suggested that the Eighth Amendment may not prohibit the use of physical force to obtain information needed to save lives; so if the United States chose to employ nonlethal torture in such an extreme case it could arguably remain in technical compliance with its treaty obligations.

A Talmudic Analysis

Do Not Stand Idly By

Text 10

Talmud, Sanhedrin 73a

מניין לרואה את חברו שהוא טובע בנהר, או חיה גוררתו,
או לסטין באין עליו שהוא חייב להצילו?

תלמוד לומר (ויקרא יט,טז): "לא תעמוד על דם רעך".

H ow do we know that if a bystander sees someone drowning in a river, being dragged by an animal, or who is being attacked by robbers that the bystander is obligated to save the victim?

Because it says, "You shall not stand by the shedding of your fellow's blood" (Leviticus 19:16).

Babylonian Talmud

A literary work of monumental proportions that draws upon the legal, spiritual, intellectual, ethical, and historical traditions of Judaism. The 37 tractates of the Babylonian Talmud contain the teachings of the Jewish sages from the period after the destruction of the 2nd Temple through the 5th century CE. It has served as the primary vehicle for the transmission of the Oral Law and the education of Jews over the centuries; it is the entry point for all subsequent legal, ethical, and theological Jewish scholarship.

Text 11

Talmud, Yoma 82a

שאין לך דבר שעומד בפני פקוח נפש חוץ מעבודה
זרה, וגילוי עריות, ושפיכות דמים.

N othing stands in the way of saving a life except for idolatry, forbidden sexual relations, and murder.

Text 12a

Rabbi David ibn Zimra, *Responsa* 627 ◫

אם אמר השלטון לישראל אמר לאחד הנח לקצץ לך אבר
אחד שאינך מת בו או אמית ישראל חבירך . . .

דכתיב דרכיה דרכי נועם (משלי ג,יז) וצריך שמשפטי תורתנו יהיו מסכימים
אל השכל והסברא; ואיך יעלה על דעתנו שיניח אדם לסמא את עינו או
לחתוך את ידו או רגלו כדי שלא ימיתו את חבירו? הלכך איני רואה טעם
לדין זה אלא מידת חסידות. ואשרי חלקו מי שיוכל לעמוד בזה.

Rabbi David ibn Zimra (Radvaz)
1479–1573

Noted halachist. Radvaz was born in Spain and immigrated to Safed, Israel upon the expulsion of the Jews from Spain in 1492. In 1513, he moved to Egypt and served as rabbi, judge, and head of the yeshivah in Cairo. He also ran many successful business ventures and was independently wealthy. In 1553, he returned to Safed where he would later be buried. He authored what would later become a classic commentary to Maimonides' code of law, and wrote many halachic responsa, of which more than ten thousand are still extant.

I f the government told a Jew, "Allow one of your limbs to be amputated—one which will not endanger your life—or we will kill your friend," [what should the Jew do]? . . .

It states, "Her ways are the ways of pleasantness" (Proverbs 3:17), and it is necessary that the laws of our Torah accord with reason and rational thought. How could it occur to us that a person should allow his eyes to be blinded or his hands or feet to be cut off so that his friend should not be killed? Therefore, I find no basis for a ruling [that obligates one to suffer the loss of a limb] other than as an act of outstanding piety. Blessed is the portion of one who can withstand this!

Text 12b

Rabbi Ya'akov Emden, *Migdal Oz, Even Bochen* 1:83

שיחויב אדם מישראל שאינו רודף להציל באחד מאיבריו את
הנרדף מזולתו, זה לא שמענו . . . גם יסורין קשים ומרים נראה
שאינו צריך לסבול בשביל הצלת חברו, דנגידא קשי ממותא.

We have not heard that an innocent person should be obliged to sacrifice a limb in order to save a victim from a pursuer. . . . Likewise, one does not need to bear severe and harsh torture in order to save another, for torture is bitterer than death.

Rabbi Ya'akov Emden (Ya'avets)
1697–1776

Talmudist and Kabbalist. Rabbi Emden was the son of Rabbi Tsvi Ashkenazi, the Chacham Tsvi. He is famed for his vocal opposition to the Sabbateans, which led to several bitter controversies. In 1728, he became rabbi of Emden, Germany, but gave up that position soon thereafter. Emden wrote many works, including a *sidur* with halachic and Kabbalistic commentary, polemical writings, halachic responsa, and glosses on the Talmud.

The Law of the Pursuer

Text 13

Maimonides, *Mishneh Torah*, Laws of the Murderer and Saving Lives 1:6–14 ▪

הרודף אחר חבירו להרגו . . . הרי כל ישראל מצווין להציל
הנרדף מיד הרודף ואפילו בנפשו של רודף.

כיצד, אם הזהירוהו והרי הוא רודף אחריו, אף על פי שלא קיבל
עליו התראה, כיון שעדיין הוא רודף, הרי זה נהרג.

ואם יכולים להצילו באבר מאיברי הרודף, כגון שיכו אותו בחץ, או
באבן, או בסייף, ויקטעו את ידו, או ישברו את רגלו, או יסמו את
עינו, עושין. ואם אינן יכולין לכוין ולא להצילו אלא אם כן הרגוהו
לרודף, הרי אלו הורגין אותו, ואף על פי שעדיין לא הרג . . .

כל היכול להציל ולא הציל עובר על "לא תעמוד על דם רעך".

Rabbi Moshe ben Maimon
(Maimonides, Rambam)
1135–1204

Halachist, philosopher, author, and physician. Maimonides was born in Cordoba, Spain. After the conquest of Cordoba by the Almohads, he fled Spain and eventually settled in Cairo, Egypt. There, he became the leader of the Jewish community and served as court physician to the vizier of Egypt. He is most noted for authoring the *Mishneh Torah*, an encyclopedic arrangement of Jewish law, and for his philosophical work, *Guide for the Perplexed*.

When a person pursues another with the intention to kill . . . we are all commanded to save the intended victim, even if it is necessary to kill the pursuer (*rodef*).

Thus, if a *rodef* is warned but continues to pursue his intended victim, even if the *rodef* did not acknowledge the warning, he should be killed.

If, however, it is possible to save the intended victim by damaging one of the pursuer's limbs—if one can strike him with an arrow, stone, or sword, and cut off his hand, break his leg, blind him—one should do so. If there is no way to save the intended victim without killing the *rodef*, one should kill him, even though the *rodef* has yet to kill. . . .

Whoever has the ability to save the victim but fails to do so, transgresses a negative commandment, (Leviticus

19:16): "You shall not stand by the shedding of your fellow's blood."

QUESTION FOR DISCUSSION

What are the implications of this text for the ticking-bomb scenario?

LEARNING EXERCISE

Based on your reading of Text 13, would you classify any of the following people as "pursuers"?

	Argument for applicability of *rodef*	Argument for inapplicability of *rodef*
The Red Brigades		
Jean Leon		
Abdul Hakim Murad		
The captured rebel leader		

The Emergency Powers

Text 14

Deuteronomy 19:15

לֹא יָקוּם עֵד אֶחָד בְּאִישׁ לְכָל עָוֹן וּלְכָל חַטָּאת בְּכָל חֵטְא אֲשֶׁר יֶחֱטָא. עַל פִּי שְׁנֵי עֵדִים אוֹ עַל פִּי שְׁלֹשָׁה עֵדִים יָקוּם דָּבָר.

A single witness shall not suffice against a person for any crime or for any wrong in connection with any offense committed. Only on the evidence of two witnesses or of three witnesses shall a charge be established.

Text 15a

Talmud, Gitin 40b

הודאת בעל דין כמאה עדים דמי.

A defendant's confession is equivalent to one hundred witnesses.

Text 15b

Maimonides, *Mishneh Torah*, Laws of the Sanhedrin 18:6 📑

גזירת הכתוב היא שאין ממיתין בית דין ולא מלקין את האדם בהודאת פיו.

It is by decree of scripture that a court can execute neither capital nor physical punishment based on a defendant's own confession.

QUESTION FOR DISCUSSION

Can you reconcile the passage of Maimonides (Text 15b) with the passage in the Talmud (Text 15a)?

Text 16a

Maimonides, *Mishneh Torah*, Laws of Kings 3:10 📑

כל ההורג נפשות שלא בראיה ברורה, או בלא התראה, אפילו בעד אחד, או שונא שהרג בשגגה, יש למלך רשות להרגו ולתקן העולם כפי מה שהשעה צריכה.

A murderer against whom the evidence is circum-stantial, or who was not warned before he slew his victim, or a murderer who was observed by only one witness, and similarly, an enemy who inadvertently killed one of his foes—the king is granted license to execute them and to improve society according to the needs of the time.

Text 16b

Maimonides, *Mishneh Torah*, Laws of the Sanhedrin 24:4–10 ▌

וכיון שרואים בית דין שפרצו העם בדבר, יש להן לגדור ולחזק הדבר כפי
מה שיראה להם, הכל הוראת שעה, לא שיקבע הלכה לדורות . . .

וכן יש לדיין לעשות מריבה עם הראוי לריב עמו, ולקללו,
ולהכותו, ולתלוש שערו . . . וכן יש לו לכפות ידים ורגלים,
ולאסור בבית האסורים, ולדחוף ולסחוב על הארץ . . .

כל אלו הדברים לפי מה שיראה הדיין שזה ראוי לכך ושהשעה צריכה.

When the court sees that the people are breaching a particular matter, they may establish safeguards to strengthen the issue according to what appears to them necessary. They may do so only as a temporary measure, as opposed to establishing these safeguards as law for all time. . . .

Similarly, a judge may enter into a controversy with a person with whom it is necessary to enter into controversy, cursing him, having him beaten, having his hair pulled out. . . . He may have a person's hands and feet bound. He may imprison him and have him pushed to the ground and dragged. . . .

All of the above should be applied according to the judge's perception of what is appropriate for the violator considering the situation at large.

Text 17a

Rabbi David ibn Zimra, on *Mishneh Torah*, Laws of Kings 3:10

ובכל הני צריך שיתבונן המלך להעמיד הדת ולתקן המעוות ולא לכבודו.

I n all of these matters, the king must have in mind to strengthen the law and correct a wrong; it should not be about his own honor.

Text 17b

Maimonides, *Mishneh Torah*, Laws of the Sanhedrin 24:10 ◧

ובכל יהיו מעשיו לשם שמים. ואל יהיה כבוד הבריות קל בעיניו.

All of the judge's deeds should be for the sake of heaven. And human dignity should not be light in the judge's eyes.

Text 18

Maimonides, *Mishneh Torah*, Laws of the Sanhedrin 24:1–2 ◧

יש לדיין לדון בדיני ממונות על פי הדברים שדעתו נוטה להן שהן אמת
והדבר חזק בלבו שהוא כן, אף על פי שאין שם ראיה ברורה . . .

כל אלו הדברים הן עיקר הדין. אבל משרבו בתי דינין שאינן הגונים,
ואפילו היו הגונים במעשיהם אינן חכמים כראוי ובעלי בינה, הסכימו רוב
בתי דיני ישראל שלא . . . ידון הדיין בסמיכת דעתו ולא בידיעתו, כדי
שלא יאמר כל הדיוט: לבי מאמין לדברי זה ודעתי סומכת על זה.

Judges may adjudicate cases involving monetary matters on factors that they are inclined to regard as true and concerning which they feels strongly in their hearts are correct, even though there is no clear proof. . . .

All of this is the normative standard of law. Nevertheless, due to the proliferation of corrupt courts and courts whose judges are not sufficiently wise or masters of understanding, the majority of the courts among the Jewish people agreed not . . . to judge according to the inclinations of one's thoughts without firm knowledge. This is to prevent a bad judge from following his heart and mind.

SHOULD THE TICKING BOMB TERRORIST BE TORTURED?
A CASE STUDY IN HOW A DEMOCRACY SHOULD MAKE TRAGIC CHOICES

ALAN M. DERSHOWITZ

"Authorizing torture is a bad and dangerous idea that can easily be made to sound plausible. There is a subtle fallacy embedded in the traditional 'ticking bomb' argument for torture to save lives."

—*Philip Heymann, former deputy attorney general*

In my nearly forty years of teaching at Harvard Law School I have always challenged my students with hypothetical and real-life problems requiring them to choose among evils. The students invariably try to resist these tragic choices by stretching their ingenuity to come up with alternative—and less tragic—options. The classic hypothetical case involves the train engineer whose brakes become inoperative. There is no way he can stop his speeding vehicle of death. Either he can do nothing, in which case he will plow into a busload of schoolchildren, or he can swerve onto another track, where he sees a drunk lying on the rails. (Neither decision will endanger him or his passengers.) There is no third choice. What should he do?

I also present my students with real-life choices from evil cases like the one that occurred in Georgia during the second decade of the twentieth century: A lawyer was told in confidence by his client that another man—a stranger to the lawyer—was about to be executed for a crime that he, the client, rather than the condemned man, had committed. The lawyer had sworn an oath not to reveal any confidential communications given to him by his clients, but to comply with that oath would make him complicit in the death of an innocent stranger. What should the lawyer (or a priest in a comparable situation) do?

Whenever I present these cases to my students, they seek, as any good lawyer should, to avoid the evils of either choice. They desperately try to break out of the rigid constraints of the hypothetical train situation by ascribing to the engineer a supermanlike ability to

drive the train off the tracks. I force them back onto the rails of my hypothetical dilemma, and they groan in frustration. Similarly, with the real-life cases, my students come up with clever options by which the lawyer can satisfy both his professional obligation of confidentiality to his client and his moral obligation not to stand idly by as the blood of his neighbor is shed. In the real case described above the lawyer tried to come up with a middle ground— with tragic consequences. He told the governor that he knew for a certainty the condemned man was innocent but that he could not disclose the source of the information. The governor commuted the death sentence to life imprisonment, whereupon the inmate was forcibly removed from the prison by a lynch mob and hanged.

Students love to debate positive choices: good, better, best. They don't mind moderately negative choices: bad, worse, worst. They hate tragic choices: unthinkable versus inconceivable.

Rational decision theory teaches us bow to choose among reasonable alternatives—good and bad— on a cost-benefit basis or on the basis of assigning weights to various choices. It does not teach us how to choose among unreasonable alternatives, each so horrible that our mind rebels even at the notion of thinking about the evil options. When I was a child we joked about a hypothetical scenario that, not surprisingly, involved a choice of evils between bodily excretions: If you were up to your neck in a vat of cat vomit and somebody threw a pile of dog poop at your face, would you duck? For those who watch TV shows like *Fear Factor* this might not seem so difficult, but for our preteen minds it was a choice of evils to be debated almost as endlessly as whether it would be worse to have to tell our parents that we (orthodox Jews who were prohibited from eating pig) had contracted trichinosis or syphilis. We actually came up with answers to these absurd hypothetical dramas (no wonder so many of us became lawyers). I will spare you the answer to the vomit-poop dilemma but reveal that the trichinosis-syphilis situation was resolved by the following sexist answer: syphilis was worse if you were a girl, trichinosis if you were a boy.

How the Current Torture Debate Began

Before September 11, 2001, no one thought the issue of torture would ever reemerge as a topic of serious debate in this country. Yet shortly after that watershed event, FBI agents began to leak stories suggesting that they might have to resort to torture to get some detainees, who were suspected of complicity in al-Qaeda terrorism, to provide information necessary to prevent a recurrence. An FBI source told the press that because "we are known for humanitarian treatment" of arrestees, we have been unable to get any terrorist suspects to divulge information about possible future plans. "We're into this thing for 35 days and nobody is talking," he said in obvious frustration. "Basically we're stuck." A senior FBI aide warned that "it could get to the spot where we could go to pressure, ... where *we won't have a choice,* and we are probably getting there."[1] But in a democracy there is *always* a choice.

In 1978 a terrorist group kidnapped Italy's former prime minister Aldo Moro and threatened to kill him. A summary of the case described the decision not to resort to torture: "During the hunt for the kidnappers of Aldo Moro, an investigator for the Italian security services proposed to General Carlo Della Chiesa [of the State Police] that a prisoner who seemed to have information on the case be tortured. The General rejected the idea, replying, 'Italy can survive the loss of Aldo Moro, but it cannot survive the introduction of torture.'" The terrorists eventually murdered Moro.[2]

The Supreme Court of Israel made the choice to disallow even moderate forms of physical pressure, despite claims that such nonlethal torture was necessary to save lives. Whether to employ any particular form of pressure on a suspect is always a matter of choice. It is the essence of democracy that we always have a choice, and we have appropriate institutional mechanisms for making choices, even—perhaps especially—choices among evils.

Constitutional democracies are, of course, constrained in the choices they may lawfully make. The Fifth Amendment prohibits compelled self-incrimination, which means that statements elicited by means of torture may not be introduced into evidence against the defendant who has been tortured.[3] But if a suspect is given immunity and then tortured into providing information about a future terrorist act, his privilege against self-incrimination has not been violated.[4] (Nor would it be violated if the information were elicited by means of "truth serum," as Judge William Webster, the former head of the FBI and the CIA, has proposed—as long as the information and its fruits were not used against him in a criminal trial.) Nor has his right to be free from "cruel and unusual punishment," since that provision of the Eighth Amendment has been interpreted to apply solely to punishment after conviction.[5] The only constitutional barriers would be the "due process" clauses of the Fifth and Fourteenth Amendments, which are quite general and sufficiently flexible to permit an argument that the only process "due" a terrorist suspected of refusing to disclose information necessary to prevent a terrorist attack is the requirement of probable cause and some degree of judicial supervision.[6]

---

[1] Walter Pincus, "Silence of 4 Terror Probe Suspects Poses a Dilemma for FBI," *Washington Post,* 10/21/2001 (emphasis added).

[2] Elizabeth Fox, "A Prosecution in Trouble," *Atlantic Monthly,* 3/1985, p. 38.

[3] But see the case of *Leon v. Wainwright 734* F.2d *no* (11th Circuit 1984), holding that a *subsequent* statement made by a man who had been *previously* tortured into revealing the whereabouts of a kidnap victim could be introduced into evidence.

[4] *Kastigar v. United States,* 406 U.S. 441 (1972).

[5] The relevant portion of the Supreme Court decision in *Ingraham v. Wright* 430 U.S. 651,664 (1977) reads: '"An examination of the history of the [Eighth] Amendment and the decisions of this Court construing the proscription against cruel and unusual punishment confirms that it was designed to protect those convicted of crimes. We adhere to this longstanding limitation."

[6] See *Leon v. Wainwright.* I have written previously on how the due process clauses could allow torture in certain circumstances. The following analysis is from Alan M. Dershowitz, "Is There a Torturous Road to Justice?" *Los Angeles Times,* 11/8/2001.

> The constitutional answer to this question may surprise people who are not familiar with the current Supreme Court interpretation of the 5th Amendment privilege against self-incrimination, which does not prohibit *any* interrogation techniques including the use of truth serum or even torture. The privilege only prohibits the *introduction into evidence* of *the fruits* of such techniques in a criminal trial against the person on whom the

In addition to possible constitutional constraints, we are also limited by our treaty obligations, which have the force of law. The Geneva Convention Against Torture prohibits all forms of torture and provides for no exceptions. It defines torture so broadly as to include many techniques that are routinely used around the world, including in Western democracies:

> For the purposes of this Convention, the term "torture" means any act by which severe pain or suffering, whether physical or mental, is intentionally inflicted on a person for such purposes as obtaining from him or a third person information or a confession, punishing him for an act he or a third person has committed or is suspected of having committed, or intimidating or coercing him or a third person, or for any reason based on discrimination of any kind, when such pain or suffering is inflicted by or at the instigation of or with the consent or acquiescence of a public official or other person acting in an official capacity.[7]

Many nations that routinely practice the most brutal forms of torture are signatories to this convention, but they hypocritically ignore it. The United States adopted the convention, but with a reservation: we agreed to be bound by it "only to the extent that it is consistent with ... the Eighth Amendment." Decisions by U.S. courts have suggested that the Eighth Amendment may not prohibit the use of physical force to obtain information needed to save lives; so if the United States chose to employ nonlethal torture in such an extreme case it could arguably remain in technical compliance with its treaty obligation. Our courts routinely refuse to apply the convention to "mental" or "psychological" torture, which is commonplace.[8]

In any event, there are legal steps we could take, if we chose to resort to torture, that would make it possible for us to use this technique for eliciting information in dire circumstances. Neither the presence nor the absence of legal constraints answers the fundamental moral question: should we? This is a choice that almost no one wants to have to make. Torture has been off the agenda of civilized discourse for so many centuries that it is a subject reserved largely for historians rather than contemporary moralists (though it remains a staple of abstract philosophers debating the virtues and vices of absolutism). I have been criticized for even discussing the issue, on the ground that academic discussion confers legitimacy on a practice that deserves none. I have also been criticized for raising a red herring, since it is "well known" that torture does not work—it produces many false confes-

---

techniques were used. Thus, if a confession were elicited from a suspect by the use of truth serum or torture, that confession—and its fruits—could not be used against that suspect. But it could be used against *another* suspect, or against *that* suspect in a non-criminal case, such as a deportation hearing.

If a suspect is given "use immunity"—a judicial decree announcing in advance that nothing the defendant says (or its fruits) can be used against him in a criminal case—he can be *compelled* to answer all proper questions. The question then becomes what sorts of pressures can constitutionally be used to implement that compulsion. We know that he can be imprisoned until be talks. But what if imprisonment is insufficient to compel him to do what he has a legal obligation to do? Can other techniques of compulsion be attempted?

Let's start with truth serum. What right would be violated if an immunized suspect who refused to comply with his legal obligation to answer questions truthfully were compelled to submit to an injection which made him do so? Not his privilege against self-incrimination, since he has no such privilege now that he has been given immunity. What about his right of bodily integrity? The involuntariness of the injection itself does not pose a constitutional barrier. No less a civil libertarian than Justice William J. Brennan rendered a decision that permitted an allegedly drunken driver to be involuntarily injected in order to remove blood for alcohol testing. Certainly there can be no constitutional distinction between an injection that *removes* a liquid and one that *injects* a liquid. What about the nature of the substance injected? If it is relatively benign and creates no significant health risk, the only issue would be that it compels the recipient to do something he doesn't want to do. But he has a legal obligation to do precisely what the serum compels him to do: answer all questions truthfully.

What if the truth serum doesn't work? Could the judge issue a "torture warrant," authorizing the FBI to employ specified forms of nonlethal physical pressure in order to compel the immunized suspect to talk? Here we run into another provision of the Constitution—the "due process" clause, which may include a general "shock the conscience" test. And torture in general certainly shocks the conscience of most civilized nations. But what if it were limited to the rare "ticking bomb" case—the situation in which a captured terrorist who knows of an imminent large-scale threat but refuses to disclose it?

---

[7] "Convention Against Torture and Other Cruel, Inhuman or Degrading Treatment or Punishment," adopted by the U.N. General Assembly, 12/10/1984, and in effect since 6/26/1987, after it was ratified by twenty nations.

[8] Samuel Francis, "Son of New World Order," *Washington Times*, 10/24/1990; *USA v. Cobb* 1 S.C.R. 587 (2001). Relevant decisions include the above-cited *Ingraham v. Wright* and *Leon v. Wainwright*.

sions and useless misinformation, because a person will say anything to stop being tortured.[9]

This argument is reminiscent of the ones my students make in desperately seeking to avoid the choice of evils by driving the hypothetical railroad train off the track. The tragic reality is that torture sometimes works, much though many people wish it did not. There are numerous instances in which torture has produced self-proving, truthful information that was necessary to prevent harm to civilians. The *Washington Post* has recounted a case from 1995 in which Philippine authorities tortured a terrorist into disclosing information that may have foiled plots to assassinate the pope and to crash eleven commercial airliners carrying approximately four thousand passengers into the Pacific Ocean, as well as a plan to fly a private Cessna filled with explosives into CIA headquarters. For sixty-seven days, intelligence agents beat the suspect "with a chair and a long piece of wood [breaking most of his ribs], forced water into his mouth, and crushed lighted cigarettes into his private parts" —a procedure that the Philippine intelligence service calls "tactical interrogation." After successfully employing this procedure they turned him over to American authorities, along with the lifesaving information they had beaten out of him.[10]

It is impossible to avoid the difficult moral dilemma of choosing among evils by denying the empirical reality that torture *sometimes* works, even if it does not always work.[11] No technique of crime prevention always works.

It is also sometimes argued that even when torture does produce accurate information that helps to foil a terrorist plot—as the Philippine torture apparently did—there is no hard evidence that the *total amount* of terrorism is thereby reduced. The foiling of any one plot may simply result in the planning of another terrorist act, especially given the unlimited reservoir of potential terrorists. This argument may have some merit in regard to recurring acts of retail terrorism, such as the suicide bombings in Israel. Preventing one bombing may not significantly reduce the total number of civilian deaths, though it does, of course, make a difference to those who would have been killed in the thwarted explosion. But the argument is much weaker when it comes to acts of mega-terrorism, such as those prevented by the Philippine torture or the attacks perpetrated on September 11, 2001. It is the prospect of such mega-acts—and the possibility of preventing them—that raises the stakes in the torture debate.

It is precisely because torture sometimes does work and can sometimes prevent major disasters that it still exists in many parts of the world and has been totally eliminated from none. It also explains why the U.S. government sometimes "renders" terrorist suspects to nations like Egypt and Jordan, "whose intelligence services have close ties to the CIA and where they can be subjected to interrogation tactics—including torture and threats to families—that are illegal in the United States," as the *Washington Post* has reported. "In some cases, U.S. intelligence agents remain closely involved in the interrogation.... 'After September 11, these sorts of movements have been occurring all of the time,' a U.S. diplomat said. 'It allows us to get information from terrorists in a way we can't do on U.S. soil.'" As former CIA counterintelligence chief Vincent Cannistraro observed: "Egyptian jails are full of guys who are missing toenails and fingernails." Our government has a "don't ask, don't tell" policy when it comes to obtaining information from other

---

[9] William F. Buckley, among others, points to the case of the person who was tortured by Philippine authorities and confessed to having taken part in the Oklahoma City bombing, but of course no one believed him. Compare this to the account described in the next paragraph of the tortured suspect whose information may have prevented a serious act of terrorism.

[10] Matthem Brzezinski, "Bust and Boom: Six Years Before the September 11 Attacks, Philippine Police Took Down an al Qaeda Cell That Had Been Plotting, Among Other Things, to Fly Explosives-Laden Planes into the Pentagon-and Possibly Some Skyscrapers," *Washington Post*, 12/30/2001. See also Alexander Cockburn, "The Wide World of Torture," *Nation*, 11/26/2001; Doug Struck, Howard Schneider, Karl Vick, and Peter Baker, "Bin Laden Followers Reach Across the Globe," *Washington Post*, 9/23/2001.

[11] There can be no doubt that torture sometimes works. Jordan apparently broke the most notorious terrorist of the 1980s, Abu Nidal, by threatening his mother. Philippine police reportedly helped crack the 1993 World Trade Center bombings by torturing a suspect. Steve Chapman, "No Tortured Dilemma," *Washington Times*, 11/15/2001. It

is, of course, possible that judicially supervised torture will work less effectively than unsupervised torture, since the torturee will know that there are limits to the torture being inflicted. At this point in time, any empirical resolution of this issue seems speculative.

---

governments that practice torture.[12] All such American complicity in foreign torture violates the plain language of the Geneva Convention Against Torture, which explicitly prohibits torture from being inflicted not only by signatory nations but also "at the instigation of or with the consent or acquiescence of" any person "acting in an official capacity." As we began to come to grips with the horrible evils of mass murder by terrorists, it became inevitable that torture would return to the agenda, and it has. The recent capture of a high-ranking al-Qaeda operative, possibly with information about terrorist "sleeper cells" and future targets, has raised the question of how to compel him to disclose this important information. We must be prepared to think about the alternatives in a rational manner. We cannot evade our responsibility by pretending that torture is not being used or by having others use it for our benefit.

Accordingly, this chapter considers torture as an example of how to think about the kinds of tragic choices we are likely to confront in the age of biological, chemical, and nuclear terrorism.

How I Began Thinking About Torture

In the late 1980s I traveled to Israel to conduct some research and teach a class at Hebrew University on civil liberties during times of crisis. In the course of my research I learned that the Israeli security services were employing what they euphemistically called "moderate physical pressure" on suspected terrorists to obtain information deemed necessary to prevent future terrorist attacks. The method employed by the security services fell somewhere between what many would regard as very rough interrogation (as practiced by the British in Northern Ireland) and outright torture (as practiced by the French in Algeria and by Egypt, the Philippines, and Jordan today). In most cases the suspect would be placed in a dark room with a smelly sack over his head. Loud, unpleasant music or other noise would blare from speakers. The suspect would be seated in an extremely uncomfortable position and then shaken vigorously until he dis-

closed the information. Statements made under this kind of nonlethal pressure could not be introduced in any court of law, both because they were involuntarily secured and because they were deemed potentially untrustworthy—at least without corroboration. But they were used as leads in the prevention of terrorist acts. Sometimes the leads proved false, other times they proved true. There is little doubt that some acts of terrorism—which would have killed many civilians—were prevented. There is also little doubt that the cost of saving these lives—measured in terms of basic human rights—was extraordinarily high.

In my classes and public lectures in Israel, I strongly condemned these methods as a violation of core civil liberties and human rights. The response that people gave, across the political spectrum from civil libertarians to law-and-order advocates, was essentially the same: but what about the "ticking bomb" case?

The ticking bomb case refers to a scenario that has been discussed by many philosophers, including Michael Walzer, Jean-Paul Sartre, and Jeremy Bentham. Walzer described such a hypothetical case in an article titled "Political Action: The Problem of Dirty Hands." In this case, a decent leader of a nation plagued with terrorism is asked "to authorize the torture of a captured rebel leader who knows or probably knows the location of a number of bombs hidden in apartment buildings across the city, set to go off within the next twenty-four hours. He orders the man tortured, convinced that he must do so for the sake of the people who might otherwise die in the explosions even though he believes that torture is wrong, indeed abominable, not just sometimes, but always."[13]

In Israel, the use of torture to prevent terrorism was not hypothetical; it was very real and recurring. I soon discovered that virtually no one was willing to take the "purist" position against torture in the ticking bomb case: namely, that the ticking bomb must be permitted to explode and kill dozens of civilians, even if this disaster could be prevented by subject-

---

[12] Rajiv Chandrasekaran and Peter Finn, "U.S. Behind Secret Transfer of Terror Suspects," *Washington Post*, 3/1112002; Kevin Johnson and Richard Willing, "Ex-CIA Chief Revitalizes 'Truth Serum' Debate," *USA Today*, 4/26/2002.

[13] Michael Walzer, "Political Action: The Problem of Dirty Hands," *Philosophy and Public Affairs*, 1973.

ing the captured terrorist to nonlethal torture and forcing him to disclose its location. I realized that the extraordinarily rare situation of the hypothetical ticking bomb terrorist was serving as a moral, intellectual, and legal justification for a pervasive *system* of coercive interrogation, which, though not the paradigm of torture, certainly bordered on it. It was then that I decided to challenge this system by directly confronting the ticking bomb case. I presented the following challenge to my Israeli audience: If the reason you permit nonlethal torture is based on the ticking bomb case, why not limit it exclusively to that compelling but rare situation? Moreover, if you believe that nonlethal torture is justifiable in the ticking bomb case, why not require advance judicial approval—a "torture warrant"? That was the origin of a controversial proposal that has received much attention, largely critical, from the media. Its goal was, and remains, to reduce the use of torture to the smallest amount and degree possible, while creating public accountability for its rare use. I saw it not as a compromise with civil liberties but rather as an effort to maximize civil liberties in the face of a realistic likelihood that torture would, in fact, take place below the radar screen of accountability.

I am not the only civil libertarian who has been stimulated into thinking about tragic choices by examining the tragic reality in Israel. At about the same time I was investigating civil liberties in Israel, the late Supreme Court justice William J. Brennan—perhaps the most committed civil libertarian in Supreme Court history—visited Israel and wrote the following:

> It may well be Israel, not the United States, that provides the best hope for building a jurisprudence that can protect civil liberties against the demands of national security, for it is Israel that has been facing real and serious threats to its security for the last forty years and seems destined to continue facing such threats in the foreseeable future....

> I [would not] be surprised if in the future the protections generally afforded civil liberties during times of world danger owed much to the lessons

Israel learns in its struggle to preserve simultaneously the liberties of its citizens and the security of its nation. For in this crucible of danger lies the opportunity to forge a worldwide jurisprudence of civil liberties that can withstand the turbulences of war and crisis.[14]

It may well be, however, that the United States should be cautious in learning from Israel. What may be right for Israel—or any small country facing terrorism—may be wrong, or not quite as right, for the world's most powerful and influential nation. When Israel takes an action, such as publicly acknowledging that it may be proper to administer nonlethal torture in the ticking bomb case, that action does not immediately become a precedent for other nations. Indeed, Israel is generally condemned, even by nations that have done, and continue to do, far worse. Its actions, even when arguably proper, result in it being characterized as an "outlaw" state. Were the United States, on the other hand, to declare its intention to allow nonlethal torture in the ticking bomb case, that declaration would effectively change international law, since our actions help define the law. Accordingly, the stakes are far higher in the debate now taking place in this country.

The Case for Torturing the Ticking Bomb Terrorist

The arguments in favor of using torture as a last resort to prevent a ticking bomb from exploding and killing many people are both simple and simple-minded. Bentham constructed a compelling hypothetical case to support his utilitarian argument against an absolute prohibition on torture:

> Suppose an occasion were to arise, in which a suspicion is entertained, as strong as that which would be received as a sufficient ground for arrest and commitment as for felony—a suspicion that at this very time a considerable number of individuals are actually suffering, by illegal violence inflictions equal in intensity to those which if in-

14 William J. Brennan, "The Quest to Develop a Jurisprudence of Civil Liberties in Times of Security Crisis," paper delivered in Jerusalem, December 22, 1987. Thanks to Einer Elhauge for bringing this to my attention.

flicted by the hand of justice, would universally be spoken of under the name of torture. For the purpose of rescuing from torture these hundred innocents, should any scruple be made of applying equal or superior torture, to extract the requisite information from the mouth of one criminal, who having it in his power to make known the place where at this time the enormity was practising or about to be practised, should refuse to do so? To say nothing of wisdom, could any pretence be made so much as to the praise of blind and vulgar humanity, by the man who to save one criminal, should determine to abandon 100 innocent persons to the same fate?[15]

If the torture of one guilty person would be justified to prevent the torture of a hundred innocent persons, it would seem to follow—certainly to Bentham—that it would also be justified to prevent the murder of thousands of innocent civilians in the ticking bomb case. Consider two hypothetical situations that are not, unfortunately, beyond the realm of possibility. In fact, they are both extrapolations on actual situations we have faced.

Several weeks before September 11,2001, the Immigration and Naturalization Service detained Zacarias Moussaoui after flight instructors reported suspicious statements he had made while taking flying lessons and paying for them with large amounts of cash.[16] The government decided not to seek a warrant to search his computer. Now imagine that they had, and that they discovered he was part of a plan to destroy large occupied buildings, but without any further details. They interrogated him, gave him immunity from prosecution, and offered him large cash rewards and a new identity. He refused to talk. They then threatened him, tried to trick him, and employed every lawful technique available. He still refused. They even injected him with sodium pentothal and other truth serums, but to no avail. The

attack now appeared to be imminent, but the FBI still had no idea what the target was or what means would be used to attack it. We could not simply evacuate all buildings indefinitely. An FBI agent proposes the use of nonlethal torture—say, a sterilized needle inserted under the fingernails to produce unbearable pain without any threat to health or life, or the method used in the film *Marathon Man,* a dental drill through an unanesthetized tooth.

The simple cost-benefit analysis for employing such nonlethal torture seems overwhelming: it is surely better to inflict nonlethal pain on one guilty terrorist who is illegally withholding information needed to prevent an act of terrorism than to permit a large number of innocent victims to die.[17] Pain is a lesser and more remediable harm than death; and the lives of a thousand innocent people should be valued more than the bodily integrity of one guilty person. If the variation on the Moussaoui case is not sufficiently compelling to make this point, we can always raise the stakes. Several weeks after September 11, our government received reports that a ten-kiloton nuclear weapon may have been stolen from Russia and was on its way to New York City, where it would be detonated and kill hundreds of thousands of people. The reliability of the source, code named Dragonfire, was uncertain, but assume for purposes of this hypothetical extension of the actual case that the source was a captured terrorist— like the one tortured by the Philippine authorities—who knew precisely how and where the weapon was being bought into New York and was to be detonated. Again, everything short of torture is tried, but to no avail. It is not absolutely certain torture will work, but it is our last, best hope for preventing a cataclysmic nuclear devastation in a city too large to evacuate in time. Should nonlethal torture be tried? Bentham would certainly have said yes.

The strongest argument against any resort to torture, even in the ticking bomb case, also derives from Bentham's utilitarian calculus. Experience has shown that if torture, which has been deemed illegitimate

---

15 Quoted in W. L. Twining and P. E. Twining, "Bentham on Torture," *Northern Ireland Legal Quarterly,* Autumn 1973, p. 347. Bentham's hypothetical question does not distinguish between torture inflicted by private persons and by governments.

16 David Johnston and Philip Shenon, "F.B.I. Curbed Scrutiny of Man Now a Suspect in the Attacks," *New York Times,* 10/6/2001.

17 It is illegal to withhold relevant information from a grand jury after receiving immunity. See *Kastigar v. U.S.* 406 U.S. 441 (1972).

by the civilized world for more than a century, were now to be legitimated—even for limited use in one extraordinary type of situation—such legitimation would constitute an important symbolic setback in the worldwide campaign against human rights abuses. Inevitably, the legitimation of torture by the world's leading democracy would provide a welcome justification for its more widespread use in other parts of the world. Two Bentham scholars, W. L. Twining and P. E. Twining, have argued that torture is unacceptable even if it is restricted to an extremely limited category of cases:

> There is at least one good practical reason for drawing a distinction between justifying an isolated act of torture in an extreme emergency of the kind postulated above and justifying the *institutionalisation* of torture as a regular practice. The circumstances are so extreme in which most of us would be prepared to justify resort to torture, if at all, the conditions we would impose would be so stringent, the practical problems of devising and enforcing adequate safeguards so difficult and the risks of abuse so great that it would be unwise and dangerous to entrust any government, however enlightened, with such a power. Even an out-and-out utilitarian can support an absolute prohibition against institutionalised torture on the ground that no government in the world can be trusted not to abuse the power and to satisfy in practice the conditions he would impose.[18]

Bentham's own justification was based on *case* or *act* utilitarianism—a demonstration that in a *particular case,* the benefits that would flow from the limited use of torture would outweigh its costs. The argument against any use of torture would derive from *rule* utilitarianism—which considers the implications of establishing a precedent that would inevitably be extended beyond its limited case utilitarian justification to other possible evils of lesser magnitude. Even terrorism itself could be justified by a case utilitarian approach. Surely one could come up with a singular situation in which the targeting of a small number of civilians could be thought necessary to save thousands of other civilians—blowing up a German kindergarten by the relatives of inmates in a Nazi death camp, for example, and threatening to repeat the targeting of German children unless the death camps were shut down.

The reason this kind of single-case utilitarian justification is simple-minded is that it has no inherent limiting principle. If nonlethal torture of one person is justified to prevent the killing of many important people, then what if it were necessary to use lethal torture—or at least torture that posed a substantial risk of death? What if it were necessary to torture the suspect's mother or children to get him to divulge the information? What if it took threatening to kill his family, his friends, his entire village?[19] Under a simple-minded quantitative case utilitarianism, anything goes as long as the number of people tortured or killed does not exceed the number that would be saved. This is morality by numbers, unless there are other constraints on what we can properly do. These other constraints can come from rule utilitarianisms or other principles of morality, such as the prohibition against deliberately punishing the innocent. Unless we are prepared to impose some limits on the use of torture or other barbaric tactics that might be of some use in preventing terrorism, we risk hurtling down a slippery slope into the abyss of amorality and ultimately tyranny. Dostoevsky captured the complexity of this dilemma in *The Brothers Karamazov* when he had Ivan pose the following question to Alyosha: "Imagine that you are creating a fabric of human destiny with the object of making men happy in the end, giving them peace at least, but that it was essential and inevitable to torture to death only one tiny creature—that baby beating its breast with its fist, for instance—and to found that edifice on its un-

---

18 Twining and Twining, "Bentham on Torture," pp. 348–49. The argument for the limited use of torture in the ticking bomb case falls into a category of argument known as "argument from the extreme case," which is a useful heuristic to counter arguments for absolute principles.

19 To demonstrate that this is not just in the realm of the hypothetical: "The former CIA officer said he also suggested the agency begin targeting close relatives of known terrorists and use them to obtain intelligence. 'You get their mothers and their brothers and their sisters under your complete control, and then you make that known to the target,' he said. 'You imply or you directly threaten [that] his family is going to pay the price if he makes the wrong decision.'" Bob Drogin and Greg Miller, "Spy Agencies Facing Questions of Tactics," *Los Angeles Times,* 10/28/2001.

avenged tears, would you consent to be the architect on those conditions? Tell me the truth."

A willingness to kill an innocent child suggests a willingness to do anything to achieve a necessary result. Hence the slippery slope.

It does not necessarily follow from this understandable fear of the slippery slope that we can never consider the use of nonlethal infliction of pain, if its use were to be limited by acceptable principles of morality. After all, imprisoning a witness who refuses to testify after being given immunity is designed to be punitive—that is painful. Such imprisonment can, on occasion, produce more pain and greater risk of death than nonlethal torture. Yet we continue to threaten and use the pain of imprisonment to loosen the tongues of reluctant witnesses.[20]

It is commonplace for police and prosecutors to threaten recalcitrant suspects with prison rape. As one prosecutor put it: "You're going to be the boyfriend of a very bad man." The slippery slope is an argument of caution, not a debate stopper, since virtually every compromise with an absolutist approach to rights carries the risk of slipping further. An appropriate response to the slippery slope is to build in a principled break. For example, if nonlethal torture were legally limited to convicted terrorists who had knowledge of future massive terrorist acts, were given immunity, and still refused to provide the information, there might still be objections to the use of torture, but they would have to go beyond the slippery slope argument.[21]

The case utilitarian argument for torturing a ticking bomb terrorist is bolstered by an argument from analogy—an *a fortiori* argument. What moral principle could justify the death penalty for past individual murders and at the same time condemn nonlethal torture to prevent future mass murders? Bentham posed this rhetorical question as support for his argument. The death penalty is, of course, reserved for convicted murderers. But again, what if torture was limited to convicted terrorists who refused to divulge information about future terrorism? Consider as well the analogy to the use of deadly force against suspects fleeing from arrest for dangerous felonies of which they have not yet been convicted. Or military retaliations that produce the predictable and inevitable collateral killing of some innocent civilians. The case against torture, if made by a Quaker who opposes the death penalty, war, self-defense, and the use of lethal force against fleeing felons, is understandable. But for anyone who justifies killing on the basis of a cost-benefit analysis, the case against the use of nonlethal torture to save multiple lives is more difficult to make. In the end, absolute opposition to torture—even nonlethal torture in the ticking bomb case—may rest more on historical and aesthetic considerations than on moral or logical ones.

In debating the issue of torture, the first question I am often asked is, "Do you want to take us back to the Middle Ages?" The association between any form of torture and gruesome death is powerful in the minds of most people knowledgeable of the history of its abuses. This understandable association makes it difficult for many people to think about nonlethal torture as a technique for *saving* lives.

The second question I am asked is, "What kind of torture do you have in mind?" When I respond by describing the sterilized needle being shoved under the fingernails, the reaction is visceral and often visible—a shudder coupled with a facial gesture of disgust. Discussions of the death penalty on the other hand can be conducted without these kinds of reactions, especially now that we literally put the condemned prisoner "to sleep" by laying him out on a gurney and injecting a lethal substance into his body. There is no breaking of the neck, burning of the brain, bursting of internal organs, or gasping for breath that used to accompany hanging, electrocution, shooting, and gassing. The executioner has been replaced by a paramedical technician, as the aesthetics of death have become more acceptable. All this tends to cover up the reality that death is forever while nonlethal

---

[20] One of my clients, who refused to testify against the mafia, was threatened by the government that if he persisted in his refusal the government would "leak" false information that he was cooperating, thus exposing him to mob retaliation.

[21] *USA v. Cobb.*

pain is temporary. In our modern age death is underrated, while pain is overrated.

I observed a similar phenomenon several years ago during the debate over corporal punishment that was generated by the decision of a court in Singapore to sentence a young American to medically supervised lashing with a cane. Americans who support the death penalty and who express little concern about inner-city prison conditions were outraged by the specter of a few welts on the buttocks of an American. It was an utterly irrational display of hypocrisy and double standards. Given a choice between a medically administrated whipping and one month in a typical state lockup or prison, any rational and knowledgeable person would choose the lash. No one dies of welts or pain, but many inmates are raped, beaten, knifed, and otherwise mutilated and tortured in American prisons. The difference is that we don't see—and we don't want to see—what goes on behind their high walls. Nor do we want to think about it. Raising the issue of torture makes Americans think about a brutalizing and unaesthetic phenomenon that has been out of our consciousness for many years. [22]

The Three—or Four—Ways

The debate over the use of torture goes back many years, with Bentham supporting it in a limited category of cases, Kant opposing it as part of his categorical imperative against improperly using people as means for achieving noble ends, and Voltaire's views on the matter being "hopelessly confused."[23] The modern resort to terrorism has renewed the debate over how a rights-based society should respond to the prospect of using nonlethal torture in the ticking bomb situation. In the late 1980s the Israeli government appointed a commission headed by a retired Supreme Court justice to look into precisely that situation. The commission concluded that there are "three ways for solving this grave dilemma between the vital need to preserve the very existence of the state and its citizens, and maintain its character as a law-abiding state." The first is to allow the security services to continue to fight terrorism in "a twilight zone which is outside the realm of law." The second is "the way of the hypocrites: they declare that they abide by the rule of law, but turn a blind eye to what goes on beneath the surface." And the third, "the truthful road of the rule of law," is that the "law itself must insure a proper framework for the activity" of the security services in seeking to prevent terrorist acts.[24]

There is of course a fourth road: namely to forgo any use of torture and simply allow the preventable terrorist act to occur.[25] After the Supreme Court of

---

22 On conditions in American prisons, see Alan M. Dershowitz, "Supreme Court Acknowledges Country's Other Rape Epidemic," *Boston Herald*, 6/12/1994.
The United States may already be guilty of violating at least the spirit of the prohibition against torture. In a recent case the Canadian Supreme Court refused to extradite an accused person to the United States because of threats made by a judge and a prosecutor regarding the treatment of those who did not voluntarily surrender themselves to the jurisdiction of the U.S. court. First, as he was sentencing a co-conspirator in the scheme, the American judge assigned to their trial commented that those fugitives who did not cooperate would get the "absolute maximum jail sentence." Then, the prosecuting attorney hinted during a television interview that uncooperative fugitives would be subject to homosexual rape in prison:

> Zubrod [prosecutor]: I have told some of these individuals, "Look, you can come down and you can put this behind you by serving your time in prison and making restitution to the victims, or you can wind up serving a great deal longer sentence under much more stringent conditions," and describe those conditions to them.
> Macintyre [reporter]: How would you describe those conditions?
> Zubrod: *You're going to be the boyfriend of a very bad man if you wait out your extradition.*
> Macintyre: And does that have much of an impact on these people?
> Zubrod: Well, out of the 89 people we've indicted so far, approximately 55 of them have said, "We give up."

After reading the transcripts, the Supreme Court of Canada held: "The pressures were not only inappropriate but also, in the case of statements made by the prosecutor on the eve of the opening of the judicial hearing in Canada, unequivocally amounted to an abuse of the

process of the court. We do not condone the threat of sexual violence as a means for one party before the court to persuade any opponent to abandon his or her right to a hearing... Nor should we expect litigants to overcome well-founded fears of violent reprisals in order to be participants in a judicial process. Aside from such intimidation itself, it is plain that a committal order requiring a fugitive to return to face such an ominous climate—which was created by those who would play a large, if not decisive role in determining the fugitive's ultimate fate—would not be consistent with the principles of fundamental justice." *USA v. Cobb* 1 S.C.R. 587 (2001). (Thanks to Craig Jones, a student, for bringing this matter to my attention.)

23 John Langbein, *Torture and the Law of Proof* (Chicago: University of Chicago Press, 1977), p. 68. Voltaire generally opposed torture but favored it in some cases.

24 A special edition of the *Israel Law Review* in 1989 presented a written symposium on the report on the Landau Commission, which investigated interrogation practices of Israel's General Security Services from 1987 to 1989.

25 A fifth approach would be simply to never discuss the issue of torture—or to postpone any such discussion until after we actually experience a ticking bomb case—but I have always believed that it is

---

Israel outlawed the use of physical pressure, the Israeli security services claimed that, as a result of the Supreme Court's decision, at least one preventable act of terrorism had been allowed to take place, one that killed several people when a bus was bombed.[26] Whether this claim is true, false, or somewhere in between is difficult to assess.[27] But it is clear that if the preventable act of terrorism was of the magnitude of the attacks of September 11, there would be a great outcry in any democracy that had deliberately refused to take available preventive action, even if it required the use of torture. During numerous public appearances since September 11, 2001, I have asked audiences for a show of hands as to how many would support the use of nonlethal torture in a ticking bomb case. Virtually every hand is raised. The few that remain down go up when I ask how many believe that torture would actually be used in such a case.

Law enforcement personnel give similar responses. This can be seen in reports of physical abuse directed against some suspects that have been detained following September 11, reports that have been taken quite seriously by at least one federal judge.[28] It is confirmed by the willingness of U.S. law enforcement officials to facilitate the torture of terrorist suspects by repressive regimes allied with our intelligence agencies. As one former CIA operative with thirty years of experience reported: "A lot of people are saying we need someone at the agency who can pull fingernails out. Others are saying, 'Let others use interrogation methods that we don't use.' The only question then is, do you want to have CIA people in the room?" The real issue, therefore, is not whether some torture would or would not be used in the ticking bomb case—it would. The question is whether it would be done openly, pursuant to a previously established legal procedure, or whether it would be done secretly, in violation of existing law.[29]

Several important values are pitted against each other in this conflict. The first is the safety and security of a nation's citizens. Under the ticking bomb scenario this value may require the use of torture, if that is the only way to prevent the bomb from exploding and killing large numbers of civilians. The second value is the preservation of civil liberties and human rights. This value requires that we not accept torture as a legitimate part of our legal system. In my debates with two prominent civil libertarians, Floyd Abrams and Harvey Silverglate, both have acknowledged that they would want nonlethal torture to be used if it

---

preferable to consider and discuss tragic choices before we confront them, so that the issue can be debated without recriminatory emotions and after-the-fact finger-pointing.

[26] "The Supreme Court of Israel left the security services a tiny window of opportunity in extreme cases. Citing the traditional common-law defense of necessity, the Supreme Court left open the possibility that a member of the security service who honestly believed that rough interrogation was the only means available to save lives in imminent danger could raise this defense. This leaves each individual member of the security services in the position of having to guess how a court would ultimately resolve his case. That is extremely unfair to such investigators. It would have been far better had the court required any investigator who believed that torture was necessary in order to save lives to apply to a judge. The judge would then be in a position either to authorize or refuse to authorize a 'torture warrant.' Such a procedure would require judges to dirty their hands by authorizing torture warrants or bear the responsibility for failing to do so. Individual interrogators should not have to place their liberty at risk by guessing how a court might ultimately decide a close case. They should be able to get an advance ruling based on the evidence available at the time.

"Perhaps the legislature will create a procedure for advance judicial scrutiny. This would be akin to the warrant requirement in the Fourth Amendment to the United States Constitution. It is a traditional role for judges to play, since it is the job of the judiciary to balance the needs for security against the imperatives of liberty. Interrogators from the security service are not trained to strike such a delicate balance. Their mission is single-minded: to prevent terrorism. Similarly, the mission of civil liberties lawyers who oppose torture is single-minded: to vindicate the individual rights of suspected terrorists. It is the role of the court to strike the appropriate balance. The Supreme Court of Israel took a giant step in the direction of striking that balance. But it—or the legislature—should take the further step of requiring the judiciary to assume responsibility in individual cases. The essence of a democracy is placing responsibility for difficult choices in a visible and neutral institution like the judiciary." Dershowitz, *Shouting Fire*, pp. 476–77.

[27] Charles M. Sennott, "Israeli High Court Bans Torture in Questioning; 10,000 Palestinians Subjected to Tactics," *Boston Globe*, 9/7/1999.

[28] Osama Awadallah, a green-card holder living in San Diego, has made various charges of torture, abuse, and denial of access to a lawyer. Shira Scheindlin, a federal district court judge in New York, has confirmed the seriousness and credibility of the charges, saying Awadallah may have been "unlawfully arrested, unlawfully searched, abused by law enforcement officials, denied access to his lawyer and family." Lewis, "Taking Our Liberties."

[29] Drogin and Miller, "Spy Agencies Facing Questions of Tactics." Philip Heymann is the only person I have debated thus far who is willing to take the position that no form of torture should ever be permitted—or used—even if thousands of lives could be saved by its use. Philip B. Heymann, "Torture Should Not Be Authorized," *Boston Globe*, 2/16/2002. Whether he would act on that principled view if he were the responsible government official who was authorized to make this life and death choice—as distinguished from an academic with the luxury of expressing views without being accountable for their consequences—is a more difficult question. He has told me that he probably would authorize torture in an actual ticking bomb case, but that it would be wrong and he would expect to be punished for it.

could prevent thousands of deaths, but they did not want torture to be officially recognized by our legal system. As Abrams put it: "In a democracy sometimes it is necessary to do things off the books and below the radar screen." Former presidential candidate Alan Keyes took the position that although torture might be *necessary* in a given situation it could never be *right*. He suggested that a president *should* authorize the torturing of a ticking bomb terrorist, but that this act should not be legitimated by the courts or incorporated into our legal system. He argued that wrongful and indeed unlawful acts might sometimes be necessary to preserve the nation, but that no aura of legitimacy should be placed on these actions by judicial imprimatur.

This understandable approach is in conflict with the third important value: namely, open accountability and visibility in a democracy. "Off-the-book actions below the radar screen" are antithetical to the theory and practice of democracy. Citizens cannot approve or disapprove of governmental actions of which they are unaware. We have learned the lesson of history that off-the-book actions can produce terrible consequences. Richard Nixon's creation of a group of "plumbers" led to Watergate, and Ronald Reagan's authorization of an off-the-books foreign policy in Central America led to the Iran-Contra scandal. And these are only the ones we know about!

Perhaps the most extreme example of such a hypocritical approach to torture comes—not surprisingly—from the French experience in Algeria. The French army used torture extensively in seeking to prevent terrorism during a brutal colonial war from 1955 to 1957. An officer who supervised this torture, General Paul Aussaresses, wrote a book recounting what he had done and seen, including the torture of dozens of Algerians. "The best way to make a terrorist talk when he refused to say what he knew was to torture him," he boasted. Although the book was published decades after the war was over, the general was prosecuted—but not for what he had done to the Algerians. Instead, he was prosecuted for *revealing* what he had done, and seeking to justify it.[30]

In a democracy governed by the rule of law, we should never want our soldiers or our president to take any action that we deem wrong or illegal. A good test of whether an action should or should not be done is whether we are prepared to have it disclosed—perhaps not immediately, but certainly after some time has passed. No legal system operating under the rule of law should ever tolerate an "off-the-books" approach to necessity. Even the defense of necessity must be justified lawfully. The road to tyranny has always been paved with claims of necessity made by those responsible for the security of a nation. Our system of checks and balances requires that all presidential actions, like all legislative or military actions, be consistent with governing law. If it is necessary to torture in the ticking bomb case, then our governing laws must accommodate this practice. If we refuse to change our law to accommodate any particular action, then our government should not take that action.[31]

Only in a democracy committed to civil liberties would a triangular conflict of this kind exist. Totalitarian and authoritarian regimes experience no such conflict, because they subscribe to neither the civil libertarian nor the democratic values that come in conflict with the value of security. The hard question

---

[30] Suzanne Daley, "France Is Seeking a Fine in Trial of Algerian War General," *New York Times*, 11/29/2001.

[31] The necessity defense is designed to allow interstitial action to be taken in the absence of any governing law and in the absence of time to change the law. It is for the nonrecurring situation that was never anticipated by the law. The use of torture in the ticking bomb case has been debated for decades. It can surely be anticipated. See Dershowitz, *Shouting Fire*, pp. 474-76.

Indeed, there is already one case in our jurisprudence in which this has occurred and the courts have considered it. In the 1984 case of *Leon v. Wainwright*, Jean Leon and an accomplice kidnapped a taxi-cab driver and held him for ransom. Leon was arrested while trying collect the ransom but refused to disclose where he was holding the victim. At this point, several police officers threatened him and then twisted his arm behind his back and choked him until he told them the victim's whereabouts. Although the federal appellate court disclaimed any wish to "sanction the use of force and coercion, by police officers" the judges went out of their way to state that this was not the act of "brutal law enforcement agents trying to obtain a confession." "This was instead a group of concerned officers acting in a reasonable manner to obtain information they needed in order to protect another individual from bodily harm or death." Although the court did not find it necessary to invoke the "necessity defense," since no charges were brought against the policemen who tortured the kidnapper, it described the torture as having been "motivated by the immediate *necessity* to find the victim and save his life." *Leon v. Wainwright* 734 F.2d 770, 772-73 (11th Circuit 1984) (emphasis added). If an appellate court would so regard the use of police brutality—torture—in a case involving one kidnap victim, it is not difficult to extrapolate to a situation in which hundreds or thousands of lives might hang in the balance.

is: which value is to be preferred when an inevitable clash occurs? One or more of these values must inevitably be compromised in making the tragic choice presented by the ticking bomb case. If we do not torture, we compromise the security and safety of our citizens. If we tolerate torture, but keep it off the books and below the radar screen, we compromise principles of democratic accountability. If we create a legal structure for limiting and controlling torture, we compromise our principled opposition to torture in all circumstances and create a potentially dangerous and expandable situation.

In 1678, the French writer Francois de La Rochefoucauld said that "hypocrisy is the homage that vice renders to virtue." In this case we have two vices: terrorism and torture. We also have two virtues: civil liberties and democratic accountability. Most civil libertarians I know prefer hypocrisy, precisely because it appears to avoid the conflict between security and civil liberties, but by choosing the way of the hypocrite these civil libertarians compromise the value of democratic accountability. Such is the nature of tragic choices in a complex world. As Bentham put it more than two centuries ago: "Government throughout is but a choice of evils." In a democracy, such choices must be made, whenever possible, with openness and democratic accountability, and subject to the rule of law.[32]

Consider another terrible choice of evils that could easily have been presented on September 11, 2001—and may well be presented in the future: a hijacked passenger jet is on a collision course with a densely occupied office building; the only way to prevent the destruction of the building and the killing of its occupants is to shoot down the jet, thereby killing its innocent passengers. This choice now seems easy, because the passengers are certain to die anyway and their somewhat earlier deaths will save numerous lives. The passenger jet must be shot down. But what if it were only *probable*, not certain, that the jet would crash into the building? Say, for example, we know from cell phone transmissions that passengers are struggling to regain control of the hijacked jet, but it

is unlikely they will succeed in time. Or say we have no communication with the jet and all we know is that it is off course and heading toward Washington, D.C., or some other densely populated city. Under these more questionable circumstances, the question becomes *who* should make this life and death choice between evils—a decision that may turn out tragically wrong?

No reasonable person would allocate this decision to a fighter jet pilot who happened to be in the area or to a local airbase commander—unless of course there was no time for the matter to be passed up the chain of command to the president or the secretary of defense. A decision of this kind should be made at the highest level possible, with visibility and accountability. Why is this not also true of the decision to torture a ticking bomb terrorist? Why should that choice of evils be relegated to a local policeman, FBI agent, or CIA operative, rather than to a judge, the attorney general, or the president?

There are, of course, important differences between the decision to shoot down the plane and the decision to torture the ticking bomb terrorist. Having to shoot down an airplane, though tragic, is not likely to be a recurring issue. There is no slope down which to slip.[33] Moreover, the jet to be shot down is filled with our fellow citizens—people with whom we can identify. The suspected terrorist we may choose to torture is a "they" —an enemy with whom we do not identify but with whose potential victims we do identify. The risk of making the wrong decision, or of overdoing the torture, is far greater, since we do not care as much what happens to "them" as to "us."[34] Finally, there is something different about torture—even nonlethal torture—that sets it apart from a quick death. In addition to the horrible history associated with torture, there is also the aesthetic of torture. The very idea of deliberately subjecting a captive human being to ex-

---

[32] Quoted in Twining and Twining, "Bentham on Torture," p. 345.

[33] For an elaboration of this view, see Dershowitz, *Shouting Fire*, pp. 97–99.

[34] The pilot who would have been responsible for shooting down the hijacked plane heading from Pennsylvania to Washington, D.C., on September 11, 2001, has praised the passengers who apparently struggled with the hijackers, causing the plane to crash. These brave passengers spared him the dreadful task of shooting down a plane full of fellow Americans. The stakes are different when it comes to torturing enemy terrorists.

cruciating pain violates our sense of what is acceptable. On a purely rational basis, it is far worse to shoot a fleeing felon in the back and kill him, yet every civilized society authorizes shooting such a suspect who poses dangers of committing violent crimes against the police or others. In the United States we execute convicted murderers, despite compelling evidence of the unfairness and ineffectiveness of capital punishment. Yet many of us recoil at the prospect of shoving a sterilized needle under the finger of a suspect who is refusing to divulge information that might prevent multiple deaths. Despite the irrationality of these distinctions, they are understandable, especially in light of the sordid history of torture.

We associate torture with the Inquisition, the Gestapo, the Stalinist purges, and the Argentine colonels responsible for the "dirty war." We recall it as a prelude to death, an integral part of a regime of gratuitous pain leading to a painful demise. We find it difficult to imagine a benign use of nonlethal torture to save lives.

Yet there was a time in the history of Anglo-Saxon law when torture was used to save life, rather than to take it, and when the limited administration of nonlethal torture was supervised by judges, including some who are well remembered in history.[35] This fascinating story has been recounted by Professor John Langbein of Yale Law School, and it is worth summarizing here because it helps inform the debate over whether, if torture would in fact be used in a ticking bomb case, it would be worse to make it part of the legal system, or worse to have it done off the books and below the radar screen.

In his book on legalized torture during the sixteenth and seventeenth centuries, *Torture and the Law of Proof,* Langbein demonstrates the trade-off between torture and other important values. Torture was employed for several purposes. First, it was used to secure the evidence necessary to obtain a guilty verdict under the rigorous criteria for conviction required at the time either the testimony of two eyewitnesses or the confession of the accused himself. Circumstantial evidence, no matter how compelling, would not do. As Langbein concludes, "no society will long tolerate a legal system in which there is no prospect in convicting unrepentant persons who commit clandestine crimes. Something bad to be done to extend the system to those cases. The two-eyewitness rule was hard to compromise or evade, but the confession invited 'subterfuge.'" The subterfuge that was adopted permitted the use of torture to obtain confessions from suspects against whom there was compelling circumstantial evidence of guilt. The circumstantial evidence, alone, could not be used to convict, but it was used to obtain a torture warrant. That torture warrant was in turn used to obtain a confession, which then had to be independently corroborated—at least in most cases (witchcraft and other such cases were exempted from the requirement of corroboration).[36]

Torture was also used against persons already convicted of capital crimes, such as high treason, who were thought to have information necessary to prevent attacks on the state.

Langbein studied eighty-one torture warrants, issued between 1540 and 1640, and found that in many of them, especially in "the higher cases of treasons, torture is used for discovery, and not for evidence." Torture was "used to protect the state" and "mostly that meant preventive torture to identify and forestall plots and plotters." It was only when the legal system loosened its requirement of proof (or introduced the "black box" of the jury system) and when perceived threats against the state diminished that torture was no longer deemed necessary to convict guilty defendants against whom there had previously been insufficient evidence, or to secure preventive information.[37]

The ancient Jewish system of jurisprudence came up with yet another solution to the conundrum of convicting the guilty and preventing harms to the community in the face of difficult evidentiary barriers. Jewish law required two witnesses and a specific ad-

---

[35] Sir Edward Coke was "designated in commissions to examine particular suspects under torture." Langbein, *Torture and the Law of Proof,* p. 73.

[36] Ibid., p. 7.
[37] Ibid., p. 90, quoting Bacon.

vance warning before a guilty person could be convicted. Because confessions were disfavored, torture was not an available option. Instead, the defendant who had been seen killing by one reliable witness, or whose guilt was obvious from the circumstantial evidence, was formally acquitted, but he was then taken to a secure location and fed a concoction of barley and water until his stomach burst and he died. Moreover, Jewish law permitted more flexible forms of self-help against those who were believed to endanger the community.[38]

Every society has insisted on the incapacitation of dangerous criminals regardless of strictures in the formal legal rules. Some use torture, others use informal sanctions, while yet others create the black box of a jury, which need not explain its common-sense verdicts. Similarly, every society insists that, if there are steps that can be taken to prevent effective acts of terrorism, these steps should be taken, even if they require some compromise with other important principles.

In deciding whether the ticking bomb terrorist should be tortured, one important question is whether there would be less torture if it were done as part of the legal system, as it was in sixteenth- and seventeenth-century England, or off the books, as it is in many countries today. The Langbein study does not definitively answer this question, but it does provide some suggestive insights. The English system of torture was more visible and thus more subject to public accountability, and it is likely that torture was employed less frequently in England than in France. "During these years when it appears that torture might have become routinized in English criminal procedure, the Privy Council kept the torture power under careful control and never allowed it to fall into the hands of the regular law enforcement officers," as it had in France. In England "no law enforcement officer… acquired the power to use torture without special warrant." Moreover, when torture warrants were abolished, "the English experiment with tor-

ture left no traces." Because it was under centralized control, it was easier to abolish than it was in France, where it persisted for many years.[39]

It is always difficult to extrapolate from history, but it seems logical that a formal, visible, accountable, and centralized system is somewhat easier to control than an ad hoc, off-the-books, and under-the-radar-screen nonsystem. I believe, though I certainly cannot prove, that a formal requirement of a judicial warrant as a prerequisite to nonlethal torture would decrease the amount of physical violence directed against suspects. At the most obvious level, a double check is always more protective than a single check. In every instance in which a warrant is requested, a field officer has already decided that torture is justified and, in the absence of a warrant requirement, would simply proceed with the torture. Requiring that decision to be approved by a judicial officer will result in fewer instances of torture even if the judge rarely turns down a request. Moreover, I believe that most judges would require compelling evidence before they would authorize so extraordinary a departure from our constitutional norms, and law enforcement officials would be reluctant to seek a warrant unless they had compelling evidence that the suspect had information needed to prevent an imminent terrorist attack. A record would be kept of every warrant granted, and although it is certainly possible that some individual agents might torture without a warrant, they would have no excuse, since a warrant procedure would be available. They could not claim "necessity," because the decision as to whether the torture is indeed necessary has been taken out of their hands and placed in the hands of a judge. In addition, even if torture were deemed totally illegal without any exception, it would still occur, though the public would be less aware of its existence.

I also believe that the rights of the suspect would be better protected with a warrant requirement. He would be granted immunity, told that he was now compelled to testify, threatened with imprisonment if he refused to do so, and given the option of providing the requested information. Only if he refused

---

[38] Din Rodef, or Law of the Pursuer, refers to the halachic principle that one may kill a person who is threatening someone else's life. This rule was set forth in the twelfth century by Moses Maimonides, a great Talmudic scholar.

[39] Langbein, *Torture and the Law of Proof,* pp.13–37, 139.

to do what he was legally compelled to do—provide necessary information, which could not incriminate him because of the immunity—would he be threatened with torture. Knowing that such a threat was authorized by the law, he might well provide the information.[40] If he still refused to, he would be subjected to judicially monitored physical measures designed to cause excruciating pain without leaving any lasting damage.

Let me cite two examples to demonstrate why I think there would be less torture with a warrant requirement than without one. Recall the case of the alleged national security wiretap placed on the phones of Martin Luther King by the Kennedy administration in the early 1960s. This was in the days when the attorney general could authorize a national security wiretap without a warrant. Today no judge would issue a warrant in a case as flimsy as that one. When Zacarias Moussaoui was detained after raising suspicions while trying to learn how to fly an airplane, the government did not even seek a national security wiretap because its lawyers believed that a judge would not have granted one. If Moussaoui's computer could have been searched without a warrant, it almost certainly would have been.

It should be recalled that in the context of searches, our Supreme Court opted for a judicial check on the discretion of the police, by requiring a search warrant in most cases. The Court has explained the reason for the warrant requirement as follows: "The informed and deliberate determinations of magistrates . . . are to be preferred over the hurried action of officers."[41] Justice Robert Jackson elaborated:

The point of the Fourth Amendment, which often is not grasped by zealous officers, is not that it denies law enforcement the support of the usual inferences which reasonable men draw from evidence. Its protection consists in requiring that those inferences be drawn by a neutral and detached magistrate instead of being judged by the officer engaged in the often competitive enterprise of ferreting out crime. Any assumption that evidence sufficient to support a magistrate's disinterested determination to issue a search warrant will justify the officers in making a search without a warrant would reduce the Amendment to nullity and leave the people's homes secure only in the discretion of police officers.[42]

Although torture is very different from a search, the policies underlying the warrant requirement are relevant to the question whether there is likely to be more torture or less if the decision is left entirely to field officers, or if a judicial officer has to approve a request for a torture warrant. As Abraham Maslow once observed, to a man with a hammer, everything looks like a nail. If the man with the hammer must get judicial approval before he can use it, he will probably use it less often and more carefully.

There are other, somewhat more subtle, considerations that should be factored into any decision regarding torture. There are some who see silence as a virtue when it comes to the choice among such horrible evils as torture and terrorism. It is far better, they argue, not to discuss or write about issues of this sort, lest they become legitimated. And legitimation is an appropriate concern. Justice Jackson, in his opinion in one of the cases concerning the detention of Japanese-Americans during World War II, made the following relevant observation:

Much is said of the danger to liberty from the Army program for deporting and detaining these citizens of Japanese extraction. But a judicial construction of the due process clause that will sustain this order is a far more subtle blow to liberty than the promulgation of the order itself. A military order, however

---

[40] When it is known that torture is a possible option, terrorists sometimes provide the information and then claim they have been tortured, in order to be able to justify their complicity to their colleagues.

[41] *U.S. v. Lefkowitz*, 285 U.S. 452, 464 (1932).
The Fourth Amendment provides that "The right of the people to be secure in their persons, houses, papers, and effects, against unreasonable searches and seizures, shall not be violated, and no Warrants shall issue, but upon probable cause, supported by Oath or affirmation, and particularly describing the place to be searched, and the persons or things to be seized." There are numerous exceptions to the warrant requirement. When there are exigent circumstances, for example, or when a person with authority consents to the search, the police do not need a warrant. Also, police officers can search someone without a warrant if they have lawfully arrested the person. If the police arrest someone inside a car, they can also search the interior of the car and any containers inside the car.

[42] *Johnson v. U.S.*, 333 U.S. 10, 13–14 (1948).

unconstitutional, is not apt to last longer than the military emergency. Even during that period a succeeding commander may revoke it all. But once a judicial opinion rationalizes such an order to show that it conforms to the Constitution, or rather rationalizes the Constitution to show that the Constitution sanctions such an order, the Court for all time has validated the principle of racial discrimination in criminal procedure and of transplanting American citizens. The principle then lies about like a loaded weapon ready for the hand of any authority that can bring forward a plausible claim of an urgent need. Every repetition imbeds that principle more deeply in our law and thinking and expands it to new purposes. All who observe the work of courts are familiar with what Judge Cardozo described as "the tendency of a principle to expand itself to the limit of its logic." A military commander may overstep the bounds of constitutionality, and it is an incident. But if we review and approve, that passing incident becomes the doctrine of the Constitution. There it has a generative power of its own, and all that it creates will be in its own image.[43]

A similar argument can be made regarding torture: if an agent tortures, that is "an incident," but if the courts authorize it, it becomes a precedent. There is, however, an important difference between the detention of Japanese-American citizens and torture. The detentions were done openly and with presidential accountability; torture would be done secretly, with official deniability. Tolerating an off-the-book system of secret torture can also establish a dangerous precedent.

A variation on this "legitimation" argument would postpone consideration of the choice between authorizing torture and forgoing a possible tactic necessary to prevent an imminent act of terrorism until after the choice—presumably the choice to torture—has been made. In that way, the discussion would not, in itself, encourage the use of torture. If it were employed, then we could decide whether it was justified, excusable, condemnable, or something in between. The problem with that argument is that no FBI agent

who tortured a suspect into disclosing information that prevented an act of mass terrorism would be prosecuted—as the policemen who tortured the kidnapper into disclosing the whereabouts of his victim were not prosecuted. In the absence of a prosecution, there would be no occasion to judge the appropriateness of the torture.

I disagree with these more passive approaches and believe that in a democracy it is always preferable to decide controversial issues in advance, rather than in the heat of battle. I would apply this rule to other tragic choices as well, including the possible use of a nuclear first strike, or retaliatory strikes—so long as the discussion was sufficiently general to avoid giving our potential enemies a strategic advantage by their knowledge of our policy.

Even if government officials decline to discuss such issues, academics have a duty to raise them and submit them to the marketplace of ideas. There may be danger in open discussion, but there is far greater danger in actions based on secret discussion, or no discussion at all.

Whatever option our nation eventually adopts—no torture even to prevent massive terrorism, no torture except with a warrant authorizing nonlethal torture, or no "officially" approved torture but its selective use beneath the radar screen—the choice is ours to make in a democracy. We do have a choice, and we should make it—before local FBI agents make it for us on the basis of a false assumption that we do not really "have a choice." We have other choices to make as well, in balancing security with liberty. It is to these choices that we now turn.

Why Terrorism Works: Understanding the Threat, Responding to the Challenge, [New Haven: Yale University Press, 2008], pp. 131–163

Reprinted with permission from the author

---

43 *Korematsu v. U.S.* 323 U.S. 214, 245–46 (1944) (Jackson, J., dissenting).

The **Rohr Jewish Learning Institute**

An affiliate of
Merkos L'Inyonei Chinuch
The Educational Arm of
The Chabad Lubavitch Movement
822 Eastern Parkway, Brooklyn, NY 11213

JEWISH LEARNING INSTITUTE

Rabbi Shraga Sherman
Merion Station, PA

Rabbi Avraham Steinmetz
S. Paulo, BR

Rabbi Avrohom Sternberg
New London, CT

Rabbi Aryeh Weinstein
Newtown, PA

Rabbi Motti Wilhelm
Portland, OR

Multimedia Development

Mrs. Rivkah Shagalow
Director

Rabbi Yisroel Silman
Creative Director

Mrs. Neria Ben Avi
Mrs. Mushka Lisker
Mrs. Rivkah Rapoport
Mrs. Chava Shapiro
Rabbi Chesky Edelman
Getzy Raskin
Moshe Raskin

Administration

Mrs. Chana Dechter

Affiliate Support

Rabbi Mendel Sirota
Mrs. Fraydee Kessler
Mrs. Mindy Wallach

Online Division

Rabbi Mendy Elishevitz
Director

Dovid Ciment
Rabbi Elchonon Korenblit
Ram Rabins
Mrs. Rochie Rivkin

Marketing and Branding

Rabbi Zalman Abraham
Director

Mrs. Shevi Rivkin
Graphic Design

Rabbi Yossi Klein
Marketing for Results

Rabbi Shmuel Loebenstein
Writer

Marketing Committee

Rabbi Simcha Backman
Glendale, CA

Rabbi Ronnie Fine
Montreal, QC

Rabbi Ovadia Goldman
Oklahoma City, OK

Rabbi Mendy Halberstam
Miami Beach, FL

Rabbi Reuven New
Boca Raton, FL

Rabbi Yehuda Shemtov
Yardley, PA

Marketing Consultants

JJ Gross
New York, NY

Warren Modlin
MednetPro, Inc.
Alpharetta, GA

Alan Rosenspan
Alan Rosenspan & Associates
Sharon, MA

Gary Wexler
Passion Marketing
Los Angeles, CA

Publication Design

Rabbi Zalman Abraham
Mendel Schtroks

Printing

Shimon Leib Jacobs
Point One Communications
Montreal, QC

Distribution

Mary Stevens
Nixa, MO

Accounting

Musie Karp
Mrs. Shaina B. Mintz
Mrs. Shulamis Nadler

JLI Departments

Rabbi Levi Kaplan
Director of Operations

Rabbi Dubi Rabinowitz
Administrator

JLI Flagship

Rabbi Yisrael Rice
Chairman
S. Rafael, CA

Rabbi Mordechai Dinerman
Rabbi Naftali Silberberg
Editors-in-Chief

Rabbi Yanky Tauber
Course Editor

Rabbi Dr. Shmuel Klatzkin
Senior Editor
Dayton, OH

Rabbi Eli Raksin
Rabbi Yanky Raskin
Associate Editors

Zeldy Nemanow
Administrative Assistant

Rabbi Mendel Sirota
Production Manager

Miriam Levy-Haim
Mrs. Naomi Saul
Mrs. Rachel Witty
Proofreaders

Department of Continuing Education

Mrs. Mindy Wallach
Director

Musie Karp
Registrar

Mrs. Shulamis Nadler
Service and Support

JLI International Desk

Rabbi Avrohom Sternberg
Chairman
New London, CT

Rabbi Dubi Rabinowitz
Director
Brooklyn, NY

Chava Farkash
Administrative Assistant

Mendel Schtroks
Content Manager

Rabbi Yosef Yitzchok Noiman
Administrator, JLI Israel
In Partnership with
Tzeirei Agudat Chabad

Rabbi Eli Wolf
Administrator, JLI in the CIS
In Parternship with the Federation of Jewish
Communities of the CIS

Rabbi Avraham Golovacheov
Regional Respresentative
German Division

Rabbi Nochum Schapiro
Regional Respresentative
Australia

Beis Medrosh L'Shluchim
in partnership with
Shluchim Exchange

Rabbi Mendy Yusewitz
Director

Rabbi Mendel Margolin
Producer

Steering Committee
Rabbi Simcha Backman
Rabbi Mendy Kotlarsky
Rabbi Efraim Mintz

JLI Academy

Rabbi Hesh Epstein
Chairman

Rabbi Yossi Klein
Director

Steering Committee
Rabbi Yoel Caroline
Rabbi Mordechai Grossbaum
Rabbi Levi Mendelow

JLI Teens
in partnership with
CTeeN: Chabad Teen Network

Rabbi Chaim Block
Chairman
San Antonio, TX

Rabbi Michoel Shapiro
Director

Mrs. Nechi Gudelsky
Program Administrators

Advisory Board

Rabbi Mendy Cohen
Merion Station, PA

Rabbi Yitzi Hein
Pittsford, NY

Rabbi Zalman Marcus
Mission Viejo, CA

Machon Shmuel
The Sami Rohr Research Institute

Rabbi Avrohom Bergstein
Dean

Rabbinic Advisory Board
Rabbi Chaim Rapoport
Rabbi Gedalya Oberlander
Rabbi Chaim Schapiro
Rabbi Levi Yitzchak Raskin
Rabbi Mordechai Farkash
Rabbi Moshe Miller
Rabbi Yossi Yaffe

Research Fellows
Rabbi Menachem Aizenman
Rabbi Yehudah Altein
Rabbi Binyomin Bitton
Rabbi Moshe Chanunu
Rabbi Yaakov Gershon
Rabbi Levi Kessler
Rabbi Nesanel Loeb
Rabbi Mendel Mellul
Rabbi Zushe Wilmowsky
Rabbi Eliezer Raksin
Rabbi Menachem Rifkind
Rabbi Mendel Zirkind
Rabbi Yehudah Dovber Zirkind

Mishnah Project

Elya Silfen
Director

myShiur:
Advanced Learning Initiative

Rabbi Shmuel Kaplan
Chairman
Potomac, MD

Rabbi Levi Kaplan
Director

National Jewish Retreat

Rabbi Hesh Epstein
Chairman
Columbia, SC

Mrs. Shaina B. Mintz
Administrator

Bruce Backman
Coordinator

Rabbi Mendy Weg
Founding Director

Rochelle Katzman
Program Coordinator

Rabbi Shmuel Karp
Shluchim Liaison

Rosh Chodesh Society

Rabbi Shmuel Kaplan
Chairman
Baltimore, MD

Mrs. Shaindy Jacobson
Director

Mrs. Chava Shapiro
Associate Director

Mrs. Fraydee Kessler
Administrator

Gitty Hanokah
Administrative Assistant

Steering Committee
Mrs. Malka Bitton
Mrs. Shula Bryski
Mrs. Rochel Holzkenner
Mrs. Devorah Kornfeld
Mrs. Chana Lipskar
Mrs. Ahuva New
Mrs. Binie Tenenbaum

Sinai Scholars Society
in partnership with Chabad on Campus

Rabbi Menachem Schmidt
Chairman
Philadelphia, PA

Rabbi Dubi Rabinowitz
Director

Devorah Leah Notik
Associate Director

Mrs. Devorah Zlatopolsky
Administrator

Executive Committee
Rabbi Moshe Chaim Dubrowski
Rabbi Yossy Gordon
Rabbi Efraim Mintz
Rabbi Menachem Schmidt
Rabbi Nechemia Vogel
Rabbi Eitan Webb
Rabbi Avi Weinstein
Dr. Chana Silberstein

Curriculum Committee
Rabbi Zalman Bluming
Rabbi Shlomie Chein
Rabbi Shlomo Rothstien

Steering Committee
Rabbi Shlomie Chein
Rabbi Moshe Laib Gray
Rabbi Dovid Gurevitch
Rabbi Mendel Matusof
Rabbi Yisroel Wilhelm

TorahCafe.com
Online Learning

Rabbi Levi Kaplan
Director

Rabbi Simcha Backman
Consultant

Rabbi Mendy Elishevitz
Rabbi Elchonon Korenblit
Website Development

Mrs. Esty Perman
Administrator

Mrs. Shirley Ruvinov
Marketing Director

Mendel Serebryanski
Content Manager

Avrohom Shimon Ezagui
Rafi Roston
Filming Crew

Moshe Levin
Elya Silfen
Video Editing

Torah Studies

Rabbi Yosef Gansburg
Chairman
Toronto, ON

Rabbi Meir Hecht
Founding Director

Rabbi Zalman Margolin
Director

Rabbi Ahrele Loschak
Managing Editor

Steering Committee
Rabbi Levi Fogelman
Rabbi Yaacov Halperin
Rabbi Nechemia Schusterman
Rabbi Ari Sollish

JLI Central
Founding Department Heads

Rabbi Mendel Bell
Brooklyn, NY

Rabbi Zalman Charytan
Acworth, GA

Rabbi Mendel Druk
Cancun, Mexico

Rabbi Menachem Gansburg
Toronto, ON

Rabbi Yoni Katz
Brooklyn, NY

Rabbi Chaim Zalman Levy
New Rochelle, NY

Rabbi Benny Rapoport
Clarks Summit, PA

Dr. Chana Silberstein
Ithaca, NY

Rabbi Elchonon Tenenbaum
Napa Valley, CA

Rohr **JLI** Faculty

ALABAMA
BIRMINGHAM
Rabbi Yossi Friedman
205.970.0100

ARIZONA
CHANDLER
Rabbi Mendel Deitsch
480.855.4333

FLAGSTAFF
Rabbi Dovie Shapiro
928.255.5756

PHOENIX
Rabbi Zalman Levertov
Rabbi Yossi Friedman
602.944.2753

SCOTTSDALE
Rabbi Yossi Levertov
480.998.1410

ARKANSAS
LITTLE ROCK
Rabbi Pinchus Ciment
501.217.0053

CALIFORNIA
AGOURA HILLS
Rabbi Moshe Bryski
Rabbi Shlomo Bistritsky
818.991.0991

ARCATA
Rabbi Eliyahu Cowen
412.390.6481

BAKERSFIELD
Rabbi Shmuli Schlanger
661.835.8381

BEL AIR
Rabbi Chaim Mentz
310.475.5311

BEVERLY HILLS
Rabbi Chaim I. Sperlin
310.734.9079

BRENTWOOD
Rabbi Boruch Hecht
Rabbi Mordechai Zaetz
310.826.4453

BURBANK
Rabbi Shmuly Kornfeld
818.954.0070

CARLSBAD
Rabbi Yeruchem Eilfort
Mrs. Nechama Eilfort
760.943.8891

CENTURY CITY
Rabbi Tzemach Cunin
310.860.1260

CHATSWORTH
Rabbi Yossi Spritzer
818.718.0777

CONTRA COSTA
Rabbi Dovber Berkowitz
925.937.4101

CORONADO
Rabbi Eli Fradkin
619.365.4728

ENCINO
Rabbi Joshua Gordon
Rabbi Aryeh Herzog
818.784.9986

FOLSOM
Rabbi Yossi Grossbaum
916.608.9811

GLENDALE
Rabbi Simcha Backman
818.240.2750

HUNTINGTON BEACH
Rabbi Aron Berkowitz
714.846.2285

IRVINE
Rabbi Alter Tenenbaum
Rabbi Elly Andrusier
949.786.5000

LA JOLLA
Rabbi Baruch Shalom Ezagui
858.455.5433

LAGUNA BEACH
Rabbi Elimelech Gurevitch
949.499.0770

LOMITA
Rabbi Eli Hecht
Rabbi Sholom Pinson
310.326.8234

LONG BEACH
Rabbi Abba Perelmuter
562.621.9828

LOS ANGELES
Rabbi Leibel Korf
323.660.5177

MARINA DEL REY
Rabbi Danny Yiftach-Hashem
Rabbi Mendy Avtzon
310.859.0770

NORTH HOLLYWOOD
Rabbi Nachman Abend
818.989.9539

NORTHRIDGE
Rabbi Eli Rivkin
818.368.3937

PACIFIC PALISADES
Rabbi Zushe Cunin
310.454.7783

PALO ALTO
Rabbi Menachem Landa
CLASSES IN HEBREW
650.322.1708

PASADENA
Rabbi Chaim Hanoka
626.564.8820

RANCHO MIRAGE
Rabbi Shimon H. Posner
760.770.7785

RANCHO PALOS VERDES
Rabbi Yitzchok Magalnic
310.544.5544

RANCHO S. FE
Rabbi Levi Raskin
858.756.7571

REDONDO BEACH
Rabbi Yossi Mintz
Rabbi Zalman Gordon
310.214.4999

SACRAMENTO
Rabbi Mendy Cohen
916.455.1400

S. BARBARA
Rabbi Zalman Kudan
CHAPTER FOUNDED BY
RABBI YOSEF LOSCHAK, OBM
805.683.1544

S. CLEMENTE
Rabbi Menachem M. Slavin
949.489.0723

S. DIEGO
Rabbi Motte Fradkin
858.547.0076

S. DIEGO-UNIVERSITY CITY
Rabbi Yudell Reiz
619.723.2439

Share the **Rohr JLI** experience with friends and relatives worldwide

S. FRANCISCO
Rabbi Shlomo Zarchi
415.752.2866

Rabbi Peretz Mochkin
415.571.8770

S. LUIS OBISPO
Rabbi Chaim Leib Hilel
805.706.0256

S. MATEO
Rabbi Yossi Marcus
Rabbi Moishe Weinbaum
650.341.4510

S. MONICA
Rabbi Boruch Rabinowitz
310.394.5699

S. RAFAEL
Rabbi Yisrael Rice
415.492.1666

SOUTH BAY
Rabbi Yosef Levin
Rabbi Ber Rosenblatt
650.424.9800

SOUTH LAKE TAHOE
Rabbi Mordechai Richler
530.314.7677

STOCKTON
Rabbi Avremel Brod
209.952.2081

STUDIO CITY
Rabbi Yossi Baitelman
818.508.6633

THOUSAND OAKS
Rabbi Chaim Bryski
805.493.7776

TUSTIN
Rabbi Yehoshua Eliezrie
714.508.2150

VENTURA
Rabbi Yakov Latowicz
Mrs. Sarah Latowicz
805.658.7441

YORBA LINDA
Rabbi Dovid Eliezrie
714.693.0770

COLORADO
ASPEN
Rabbi Mendel Mintz
970.544.3770

DENVER
Rabbi Mendel Popack
720.515.4337

Rabbi Yossi Serebryanski
303.744.9699

FORT COLLINS
Rabbi Yerachmiel Gorelik
970.407.1613

HIGHLANDS RANCH
Rabbi Avraham Mintz
303.694.9119

LONGMONT
Rabbi Yakov Dovid Borenstein
303.678.7595

VAIL
Rabbi Dovid Mintz
970.476.7887

WESTMINSTER
Rabbi Benjy Brackman
303.429.5177

CONNECTICUT
GREENWICH
Rabbi Yossi Deren
Rabbi Menachem Feldman
203.629.9059

NEW HAVEN
Rabbi Yosef Y. Hodakov
203.795.5261

NEW LONDON
Rabbi Avrohom Sternberg
860.437.8000

STAMFORD
Rabbi Yisrael Deren
Rabbi Levi Mendelow
203.3.CHABAD

WEST HARTFORD
Rabbi Yosef Gopin
Rabbi Shaya Gopin
860.659.2422

WESTPORT
Rabbi Yehuda L. Kantor
Mrs. Dina Kantor
203.226.8584

DELAWARE
WILMINGTON
Rabbi Chuni Vogel
302.529.9900

FLORIDA
BAL HARBOUR
Rabbi Dov Schochet
305.868.1411

BOCA RATON
Rabbi Zalman Bukiet
Rabbi Moishe Denburg
Rabbi Arele Gopin
561.417.7797

BOYNTON BEACH
Rabbi Yosef Yitzchok Raichik
561.732.4633

BRADENTON
Rabbi Menachem Bukiet
941.388.9656

CAPE CORAL
Rabbi Yossi Labkowski
239.541.1777

CORAL GABLES
Rabbi Avrohom Stolik
305.490.7572

CORAL SPRINGS
Rabbi Yankie Denburg
954.471.8646

DELRAY BEACH
Rabbi Sholom Ber Korf
561.496.6228

EAST BOCA RATON
Rabbi Ruvi New
561.417.7797

FORT LAUDERDALE
Rabbi Yitzchok Naparstek
954.568.1190

FORT MYERS
Rabbi Yitzchok Minkowicz
Mrs. Nechama Minkowicz
239.433.7708

HOLLYWOOD
Rabbi Leizer Barash
954.965.9933

KENDALL
Rabbi Yossi Harlig
305.234.5654

LAKELAND
Rabbi Moshe Lazaros
863.510.5968

LAKE MARY
Rabbi Yanky Majesky
407.878.3011

MIAMI BEACH
Rabbi Shragi Mann
786.264.1111

MIAMI–MIDTOWN
Rabbi Shmuel Gopin
305.573.9995

OCALA
Rabbi Yossi Hecht
352.291.2218

ORLANDO
Rabbi Yosef Konikov
407.354.3660

PALM BEACH GARDENS
Rabbi Dovid Vigler
561.624.2223

PALMETTO BAY
Rabbi Zalman Gansburg
786.282.0413

PLANTATION
Rabbi Pinchas Taylor
954.644.9177

PONTE VEDRA BEACH
Rabbi Nochum Kurinsky
904.543.9301

SARASOTA
Rabbi Chaim Shaul Steinmetz
941.925.0770

SATELLITE BEACH
Rabbi Zvi Konikov
321.777.2770

SOUTH PALM BEACH
Rabbi Leibel Stolik
561.889.3499

SOUTH TAMPA
Rabbi Mendy Dubrowski
813.287.1795

SUNNY ISLES BEACH
Rabbi Alexander Kaller
305.803.5315

WESTON
Rabbi Yisroel Spalter
954.349.6565

WEST PALM BEACH
Rabbi Yoel Gancz
561.659.7770

VENICE
Rabbi Sholom Ber Schmerling
941.493.2770

GEORGIA
ALPHARETTA
Rabbi Hirshy Minkowicz
770.410.9000

ATLANTA
Rabbi Yossi New
Rabbi Isser New
404.843.2464

ATLANTA: INTOWN
Rabbi Eliyahu Schusterman
Rabbi Ari Sollish
404.898.0434

GWINNETT
Rabbi Yossi Lerman
678.595.0196

MARIETTA
Rabbi Ephraim Silverman
770.565.4412

IDAHO
BOISE
Rabbi Mendel Lifshitz
208.853.9200

ILLINOIS
CHAMPAIGN
Rabbi Dovid Tiechtel
217.355.8672

CHICAGO
Rabbi Meir Hecht
312.714.4655

Rabbi Yosef Moscowitz
773.772.3770

Rabbi Levi Notik
773.274.5123

CHICAGO-HYDE PARK
Rabbi Yossi Brackman
773.955.8672

GLENVIEW
Rabbi Yishaya Benjaminson
847.998.9896

HIGHLAND PARK
Mrs. Michla Schanowitz
847.266.0770

NAPERVILLE
Rabbi Mendy Goldstein
630.778.9770

NORTHBROOK
Rabbi Meir Moscowitz
847.564.8770

Rabbi Menachem Slavaticki
CLASSES IN HEBREW
847.350.9770

OAK PARK
Rabbi Yitzchok Bergstein
708.524.1530

PEORIA
Rabbi Eli Langsam
309.692.2250

ROCKFORD
Rabbi Yecheskel Rothman
815.596.0032

SKOKIE
Rabbi Yochanan Posner
847.677.1770

WILMETTE
Rabbi Dovid Flinkenstein
847.251.7707

INDIANA
INDIANAPOLIS
Rabbi Mendel Schusterman
317.251.5573

KANSAS
OVERLAND PARK
Rabbi Mendy Wineberg
913.649.4852

KENTUCKY
LOUISVILLE
Rabbi Avrohom Litvin
502.459.1770

LOUISIANA
METAIRIE
Rabbi Yossie Nemes
Rabbi Mendel Ceitlin
504.454.2910

MARYLAND
BALTIMORE
Rabbi Elchonon Lisbon
410.358.4787

Rabbi Velvel Belinsky
CLASSES IN RUSSIAN
410.764.5000

BEL AIR
Rabbi Yekusiel Schusterman
443.353.9718

BETHESDA
Rabbi Bentzion Geisinsky
Rabbi Sender Geisinsky
301.913.9777

COLUMBIA
Rabbi Hillel Baron
Rabbi Yosef Chaim Sufrin
410.740.2424

FREDERICK
Rabbi Boruch Labkowski
301.996.3659

GAITHERSBURG
Rabbi Sholom Raichik
301.926.3632

OLNEY
Rabbi Bentzy Stolik
301.660.6770

OWINGS MILLS
Rabbi Nochum H. Katsenelenbogen
410.356.5156

POTOMAC
Rabbi Mendel Bluming
301.983.4200

Rabbi Mendel Kaplan
301.983.1485

ROCKVILLE
Rabbi Moishe Kavka
301.836.1242

MASSACHUSETTS
ANDOVER
Rabbi Asher Bronstein
Rabbi Zalman Borenstein
978.470.2288

CAPE COD
Rabbi Yekusiel Alperowitz
508.775.2324

CHESTNUT HILL
Rabbi Mendy Uminer
617.738.9770

LONGMEADOW
Rabbi Yakov Wolff
413.567.8665

NEWTON
Rabbi Shalom Ber Prus
617.244.1200

MILFORD
Rabbi Mendy Kievman
508.473.1299

SUDBURY
Rabbi Yisroel Freeman
978.443.3691

SWAMPSCOTT
Mrs. Layah Lipsker
781.581.3833

MICHIGAN
ANN ARBOR
Rabbi Aharon Goldstein
734.995.3276

GRAND RAPIDS
Rabbi Mordechai Haller
616.957.0770

Share the **Rohr JLI** experience with friends and relatives worldwide

WEST BLOOMFIELD
Rabbi Elimelech Silberberg
248.855.6170

MINNESOTA
MINNETONKA
Rabbi Mordechai Grossbaum
952.929.9922

S. PAUL
Rabbi Shneur Zalman Bendet
651.278.8401

MISSOURI
S. LOUIS
Rabbi Yosef Landa
314.725.0400

MONTANA
BOZEMAN
Rabbi Chaim Shaul Bruk
406.585.8770

NEVADA
SUMMERLIN
Rabbi Yisroel Schanowitz
Rabbi Tzvi Bronchtain
702.855.0770

NEW JERSEY
BASKING RIDGE
Rabbi Mendy Herson
908.604.8844

CHERRY HILL
Rabbi Mendy Mangel
856.874.1500

CLINTON
Rabbi Eli Kornfeld
908.623.7000

FAIR LAWN
Rabbi Avrohom Bergstein
718.839.5296

FANWOOD
Rabbi Avrohom Blesofsky
908.790.0008

FORT LEE
Rabbi Meir Konikov
201.886.1238

FRANKLIN LAKES
Rabbi Chanoch Kaplan
201.848.0449

HASKELL
Rabbi Mendy Gurkov
201.696.7609

HILLSBOROUGH
Rabbi Shmaya Krinsky
908.874.0444

HOLMDEL
Rabbi Shmaya Galperin
732.772.1998

MADISON
Rabbi Shalom Lubin
973.377.0707

MANALAPAN
Rabbi Boruch Chazanow
Rabbi Levi Wolosow
732.972.3687

MEDFORD
Rabbi Yitzchok Kahan
609.953.3150

MOUNTAIN LAKES
Rabbi Levi Dubinsky
973.551.1898

MULLICA HILL
Rabbi Avrohom Richler
856.733.0770

NORTH BRUNSWICK
Rabbi Levi Azimov
732.398.9492

OLD TAPPAN
Rabbi Mendy Lewis
201.767.4008

ROCKAWAY
Rabbi Asher Herson
Rabbi Mordechai Baumgarten
973.625.1525

TEANECK
Rabbi Ephraim Simon
201.907.0686

TENAFLY
Rabbi Mordechai Shain
Rabbi Yitzchak Gershovitz
201.871.1152

TOMS RIVER
Rabbi Moshe Gourarie
732.349.4199

WEST ORANGE
Rabbi Mendy Kasowitz
973.486.2362

WOODCLIFF LAKE
Rabbi Dov Drizin
201.476.0157

NEW MEXICO
S. FE
Rabbi Berel Levertov
505.983.2000

NEW YORK
BEDFORD
Rabbi Arik Wolf
914.666.6065

BINGHAMTON
Mrs. Rivkah Slonim
607.797.0015

BRIGHTON BEACH
Rabbi Zushe Winner
Rabbi Moshe Winner
718.946.9833

BRONXVILLE
Rabbi Sruli Deitsch
917.755.0078

BROOKLYN HEIGHTS
Rabbi Mendy Hecht
Rabbi Ari Raskin
347.378.2641

CEDARHURST
Rabbi Zalman Wolowik
516.295.2478

CHESTNUT RIDGE
Rabbi Chaim Tzvi Ehrenreich
845.356.6686

COMMACK
Rabbi Mendel Teldon
631.543.3343

DIX HILLS
Rabbi Yaakov Saacks
631.351.8672

DOBBS FERRY
Rabbi Benjy Silverman
914.693.6100

EAST HAMPTON
Rabbi Leibel Baumgarten
Rabbi Mendy Goldberg
631.329.5800

FOREST HILLS
Rabbi Yossi Mendelson
917.861.9726

GREAT NECK
Rabbi Yoseph Geisinsky
516.487.4554

ITHACA
Rabbi Eli Silberstein
607.257.7379

KINGSTON
Rabbi Yitzchok Hecht
845.334.9044

LARCHMONT
Rabbi Mendel Silberstein
914.834.4321

LONG BEACH
Rabbi Eli Goodman
516.897.2473

NYC KEHILATH JESHURUN
Rabbi Elie Weinstock
212.774.5636

NYC TRIBECA
Rabbi S. Zalman Paris
646.510.3109

OSSINING
Rabbi Dovid Labkowski
914.923.2522

PORT WASHINGTON
Rabbi Shalom Paltiel
516.767.8672

RIVERDALE
Rabbi Levi Shemtov
718.549.1100

Share the **Rohr JLI** experience with friends and relatives worldwide

ROCHESTER
Rabbi Nechemia Vogel
585.271.0330

ROSLYN
Rabbi Yaakov Reiter
516.484.8185

SEA GATE
Rabbi Chaim Brikman
718.266.1736

Rabbi Nachman Segal
CLASSES IN HEBREW
718.761.4483

STONY BROOK
Rabbi Shalom Ber Cohen
631.585.0521

SUFFERN
Rabbi Shmuel Gancz
845.368.1889

WESTBURY
Rabbi Mendy Brownstein
516.850.4486

NORTH CAROLINA
ASHEVILLE
Rabbi Shaya Susskind
828.505.0746

CARYY
Rabbi Yisroel Cotlar
919.651.9710

CHAPEL HILL
Rabbi Zalman Bluming
919.630.5129

CHARLOTTE
Rabbi Yossi Groner
Rabbi Shlomo Cohen
704.366.3984

GREENSBORO
Rabbi Yosef Plotkin
336.617.8120

RALEIGH
Rabbi Pinchas Herman
Rabbi Lev Cotlar
919.637.6950

WILMINGTON
Rabbi Moshe Lieblich
910.763.4770

NORTH DAKOTA
FARGO
Rabbi Yonah Grossman
701.212.4164

OHIO
BEACHWOOD
Rabbi Shmuli Friedman
Rabbi Moshe Gancz
216.370.2887

BLUE ASH
Rabbi Yisroel Mangel
513.793.5200

COLUMBUS
Rabbi Areyah Kaltmann
Rabbi Levi Andrusier
614.294.3296

OKLAHOMA
OKLAHOMA CITY
Rabbi Ovadia Goldman
405.524.4800

TULSA
Rabbi Yehuda Weg
918.492.4499

OREGON
PORTLAND
Rabbi Moshe Wilhelm
Rabbi Mordechai Wilhelm
503.977.9947

SALEM
Rabbi Avrohom Yitzchok Perlstein
503.383.9569

PENNSYLVANIA
AMBLER
Rabbi Shaya Deitsch
215.591.9310

BALA CYNWYD
Rabbi Shraga Sherman
610.660.9192

LAFAYETTE HILL
Rabbi Yisroel Kotlarsky
347.526.1430

LANCASTER
Rabbi Elazar Green
717.368.6565

MEDIA
Rabbi Eli Dovid Strasberg
610.543.5095

NEWTOWN
Rabbi Aryeh Weinstein
215.497.9925

PHILADELPHIA: CENTER CITY
Rabbi Yochonon Goldman
215.238.2100

PITTSBURGH
Rabbi Yisroel Altein
412.422.7300 ext. 269

PITTSBURGH: SOUTH HILLS
Rabbi Mendy Rosenblum
412.278.3693

RYDAL
Rabbi Zushe Gurevitz
215.572.1511

WYNNEWOOD
Rabbi Moishe Brennan
610.529.9011

RHODE ISLAND
WARWICK
Rabbi Yossi Laufer
401.884.7888

SOUTH CAROLINA
COLUMBIA
Rabbi Hesh Epstein
803.782.1831

TENNESSEE
CHATTANOOGA
Rabbi Shaul Perlstein
423.490.1106

KNOXVILLE
Rabbi Yossi Wilhelm
865.588.8584

MEMPHIS
Rabbi Levi Klein
901.766.1800

TEXAS
ARLINGTON
Rabbi Levi Gurevitch
817.451.1171

DALLAS
Rabbi Peretz Shapiro
Rabbi Moshe Naparstek
972.818.0770

FORT WORTH
Rabbi Dov Mandel
817.263.7701

HOUSTON
Rabbi Moishe Traxler
713.774.0300

HOUSTON: RICE UNIVERSITY AREA
Rabbi Eliezer Lazaroff
713.522.2004

LEAGUE CITY
Rabbi Yitzchok Schmukler
713.398.2460

PLANO
Rabbi Mendel Block
Rabbi Yehudah Horowitz
972.596.8270

S. ANTONIO
Rabbi Chaim Block
Rabbi Levi Teldon
210.492.1085

THE WOODLANDS
Rabbi Mendel Blecher
281.719.5213

UTAH
SALT LAKE CITY
Rabbi Benny Zippel
801.467.7777

VERMONT
BURLINGTON
Rabbi Yitzchok Raskin
802.658.5770

VIRGINIA
ALEXANDRIA/ARLINGTON
Rabbi Mordechai Newman
703.370.2774

FAIRFAX
Rabbi Leibel Fajnland
703.426.1980

NORFOLK
Rabbi Aaron Margolin
Rabbi Levi Brashevitzky
757.616.0770

RICHMOND
Rabbi Shlomo Pereira
804.740.2000

TYSONS CORNER
Rabbi Chezzy Deitsch
CHAPTER FOUNDED BY
RABBI LEVI DEITSCH, OBM
703.829.5770

WASHINGTON
OLYMPIA
Rabbi Cheski Edelman
360.584.4306

SEATTLE
Rabbi Elazar Bogomilsky
206.527.1411

SPOKANE COUNTY
Rabbi Yisroel Hahn
509.443.0770

WISCONSIN
MADISON
Rabbi Avremel Matusof
608.231.3450

MILWAUKEE
Rabbi Mendel Shmotkin
414.961.6100

WAUKESHA
Rabbi Levi Brook
925.708.4203

PUERTO RICO
CAROLINA
Rabbi Mendel Zarchi
787.253.0894

ARGENTINA
BUENOS AIRES
Rabbi Mendel Levy
Rabbi Shlomo Levy
54.11.4807.2223

CAPITAL FEDERAL
Rabbi Mendy Gurevitch
54.11.4545.7771

PALERMO NUEVO
Rabbi Mendy Grunblatt
54.11.4772.1024

RECOLETA
Rabbi Hirshel Hendel
54.11.4807.7073

AUSTRALIA
AUSTRALIAN CAPITAL TERRITORY
CANBERRA
Rabbi Shmuel Feldman
614.3167.7805

NEW SOUTH WALES
BONDI BEACH
Rabbi Aron Moss
612.8005.6613

DOUBLE BAY
Rabbi Yanky Berger
Rabbi Yisroel Dolnikov
612.9327.1644

DOVER HEIGHTS
Rabbi Motti Feldman
612.9387.3822

NORTH SHORE
Rabbi Nochum Schapiro
Mrs. Fruma Schapiro
612.9488.9548

RANDWICK
Rabbi Aryeh Leib Solomon
613.9375.1600

SOUTH HEAD
Rabbi Benzion Milecki
612.9337.6775

QUEENSLAND
BRISBANE
Rabbi Levi Jaffe
617.3843.6770

SOUTH AUSTRALIA
GLENSIDE
Rabbi Yossi Engel
618.8338.2922

VICTORIA
BENTLEIGH EAST
Rabbi Mendel Raskin
613.9570.6707

CAULFIELD SOUTH
Rabbi Peretz Schapiro
613.9532.9180

ELSTERNWICK
Rabbi Chaim Cowen
614.3330.8584

Rabbi Motty Liberow
613.9533.0090

MALVERN
Rabbi Zev Slavin
614.0476.6759

Rabbi Shimshon Yurkowicz
613.9822.3600

MELBOURNE
Rabbi Mendel Groner
613.9532.7299

Rabbi Dovid Gutnick
614.3038.4948

MOORABBIN
Rabbi Elisha Greenbaum
614.0349.0434

WESTERN AUSTRALIA
PERTH
Rabbi Shalom White
618.9275.2106

BELARUS
GRODNO
Rabbi Yitzchak Kofman
375.29.644.3690

BRAZIL
RIO DE JANEIRO
Rabbi Avrohom Tsvi Beuthner
Rabbi Yehoshua Binyomin Goldman
55.21.2294.3138

S. PAULO
Rabbi Avraham Steinmetz
55.11.3081.3081

CANADA
ALBERTA
CALGARY
Rabbi Mordechai Groner
403.238.4880

EDMONTON
Rabbi Ari Drelich
Rabbi Mendy Blachman
780.851.1515

BRITISH COLUMBIA
RICHMOND
Rabbi Yechiel Baitelman
604.277.6427

VANCOUVER
Rabbi Yitzchok Wineberg
604.266.1313

VICTORIA
Rabbi Meir Kaplan
250.595.7656

MANITOBA
WINNIPEG
Rabbi Avrohom Altein
Rabbi Shmuel Altein
204.339.8737

NOVA SCOTIA
HALIFAX
Rabbi Mendel Feldman
902.422.4222

ONTARIO
HAMILTON
Rabbi Chanoch Rosenfeld
905.529.7458

LAWRENCE/EGLINTON
Rabbi Menachem Gansburg
416.546.8770

LONDON
Rabbi Eliezer Gurkow
519.434.3962

MISSISSAUGA
Rabbi Yitzchok Slavin
905.820.4432

NIAGARA FALLS
Rabbi Zalman Zaltzman
905.356.7200

OTTAWA
Rabbi Menachem M. Blum
613.823.0866

RICHMOND HILL
Rabbi Mendel Bernstein
905.770.7700

Rabbi Yossi Hecht
905.773.6477

TORONTO AREA BJL
Rabbi Leib Chaiken
416.916.7202

GREATER TORONTO
REGIONAL OFFICE & THORNHILL
Rabbi Yossi Gansburg
905.731.7000

YORK MILLS
Rabbi Levi Gansburg
647.345.3800

WATERLOO
Rabbi Moshe Goldman
226.338.7770

WHITBY
Rabbi Tzali Borenstein
905.493.9007

QUEBEC
MONTREAL
Rabbi Ronnie Fine
Pesach Nussbaum
514.342.3.JLI

Rabbi Levi Y New
514.739.0770

TOWN OF MOUNT ROYAL
Rabbi Moshe Krasnanski
Rabbi Shneur Zalman Rader
514.739.0770

VILLE S. LAURENT
Rabbi Schneur Zalmen Silberstein
514.808.1418

WESTMOUNT
Rabbi Yossi Shanowitz
Mrs. Devorah Leah Shanowitz
514.937.4772

SASKATCHEWAN
SASKATOON
Rabbi Raphael Kats
306.384.4370

CAYMAN ISLAND
GRAND CAYMAN
Rabbi Berel Pewzner
717.798.1040

COLOMBIA
BOGOTA
Rabbi Yehoshua B. Rosenfeld
Rabbi Chanoch Piekarski
571.635.8251

DENMARK
COPENHAGEN
Rabbi Yitzchok Lowenthal
45.3316.1850

ESTONIA
TALLINN
Rabbi Shmuel Kot
372.662.30.50

GEORGIA
TBILISI
Rabbi Meir Kozlovsky
995.593.23.91.15

GERMANY
BERLIN
Rabbi Yehuda Tiechtel
49.30.2128.0830

COLOGNE
Rabbi Mendel Schtroks
49.22.1240.3902

DUSSELDORF
Rabbi Chaim Barkahn
49.21.1420.9693

HAMBURG
Rabbi Shlomo Bistriztsky
49.40.4142.4190

MUNICH
Rabbi Yochonon Gordon
49.89.4190.2812

GREECE
ATHENS
Rabbi Mendel Hendel
30.210.520.2880

GUATEMALA
GUATEMALA CITY
Rabbi Shalom Pelman
502.2485.0770

ISRAEL
ASHKELON
Rabbi Shneor Lieberman
054.977.0512

BALFURYA
Rabbi Noam Bar-Tov
054.580.4770

CAESAREA
Rabbi Chaim Meir Lieberman
054.621.2586

EVEN YEHUDA
Rabbi Menachem Noyman
054.777.0707

GANEI TIKVA
Rabbi Gershon Shnur
054.524.2358

GIV'ATAYIM
Rabbi Pinchus Bitton
052.643.8770

HAIFA
Rabbi Yehuda Dunin
054.426.3763

KARMIEL
Rabbi Mendy Elishevitz
054.521.3073

KFAR SABBA
Rabbi Yossi Baitch
054.445.5020

KIRYAT BIALIK
Rabbi Pinny Marton
050.661.1768

KIRYAT MOTZKIN
Rabbi Shimon Eizenbach
050.902.0770

KOCHAV YAIR
Rabbi Dovi Greenberg
054.332.6244

MACCABIM RE'UT
Rabbi Yosef Yitzchak Noiman
054.977.0549

MODIIN
Rabbi Boruch Slonim
054.300.1770

NES ZIYONA
Rabbi Menachem Feldman
054.497.7092

NETANYA
Rabbi Schneur Brod
054.579.7572

RAMAT GAN-KRINITZI
Rabbi Yisroel Gurevitz
052.743.2814

RAMAT GAN-MAROM NAVE
Rabbi Binyamin Meir Kali
050.476.0770

RAMAT YISHAI
Rabbi Shneor Zalman Wolosow
052.324.5475

RISHON LEZION
Rabbi Uri Keshet
050.722.4593

ROSH PINA
Rabbi Sholom Ber Hertzel
052.458.7600

YEHUD
Rabbi Shmuel Wolf
053.536.1479

Share the **Rohr JLI** experience with friends and relatives worldwide

ITALY
FIRENZE
Rabbi Levi Wolvovsky
39.389.595.2034

KAZAKHSTAN
ALMATY
Rabbi Shevach Zlatopolsky
7.7272.77.59.77

LATVIA
RIGA
Rabbi Shneur Zalman Kot
371.6733.1520

NETHERLANDS
DEN HAAG
Rabbi Shmuel Katzman
31.70.347.0222

NOORD-HOLLAND
AMSTERDAM
Rabbi Yanki Jacobs
31.6.4498.8627

PANAMA
PANAMA CITY
Rabbi Ari Laine
Rabbi Gabriel Benayon
507.223.3383

RUSSIA
ASTRAKHAN
Rabbi Yisroel Melamed
7.851.239.28.24

BRYANSK
Rabbi Menachem Mendel Zaklas
7.483.264.55.15

CHELYABINSK
Rabbi Meir Kirsh
7.351.263.24.68

MOSCOW-MARINA ROSHA
Rabbi Mordechai Weisberg
7.495.645.50.00

MOSCOW-SOKOLNIKI
Rabbi Avraham Bekerman
7.495.660.07.70

NIZHNY NOVGOROD
Rabbi Shimon Bergman
7.920.253.47.70

OMSK
Rabbi Osher Krichevsky
7.381.231.33.07

PERM
Rabbi Zalman Deutch
7.342.212.47.32

SAMARA
Rabbi Shlomo Deutch
7.846.333.40.64

SARATOV
Rabbi Yaakov Kubitshek
7.8452.21.58.00

S. PETERSBURG
Rabbi Zvi Pinsky
7.812.713.62.09

ROSTOV
Rabbi Chaim Danzinger
7.8632.99.02.68

TOGLIATTI
Rabbi Meier Fischer
7.848.273.02.84

UFA
Rabbi Dan Krichevsky
7.347.244.55.33

VORONEZH
Rabbi Levi Stiefel
7.473.252.96.99

SINGAPORE
SINGAPORE
Rabbi Mordechai Abergel
656.337.2189

Rabbi Netanel Rivni
CLASSES IN HEBREW
656.336.2127

SOUTH AFRICA
CAPE TOWN
Rabbi Mendel Popack
Rabbi Pinchas Hecht
27.21.434.3740

JOHANNESBURG
Rabbi Dovid Hazdan
Rabbi Shmuel Simpson
27.11.728.8152

Rabbi Dovid Masinter
Rabbi Ari Kievman
27.11.440.6600

SWEDEN
STOCKHOLM
Rabbi Chaim Greisman
468.679.7067

SWITZERLAND
BASEL
Rabbi Zalman Wishedski
41.76.559.9236

LUGANO
Rabbi Yaakov Tzvi Kantor
41.91.921.3720

LUZERN
Rabbi Chaim Drukman
41.41.361.1770

UKRAINE
CHERKASSY
Rabbi Dov Axelrod
380.472.45.7080

DNEPROPETROVSK
Rabbi Dan Makagon
380.504.51.13.18

NIKOLAYEV
Rabbi Sholom Gotlieb
380.512.37.37.71

ZHITOMIR
Rabbi Shlomo Wilhelm
380.504.63.01.32

ODESSA
Rabbi Avraham Wolf
Rabbi Yaakov Neiman
38.048.728.0770 ext. 280

UNITED KINGDOM
EDGEWARE
Rabbi Leivi Sudak
Rabbi Yaron Jacobs
44.208.905.4141

LEEDS
Rabbi Eli Pink
44.113.266.3311

LONDON
Rabbi Gershon Overlander
Rabbi Dovid Katz
44.208.202.1600

Rabbi Nissan D. Dubov
44.20.8944.1581

MANCHESTER
Rabbi Akiva Cohen
Rabbi Levi Cohen
44.161.740.4243

URUGUAY
MONTEVIDEO
Rabbi Eliezer Shemtov
598.2.709.3444

VENEZUELA
CARACAS
Rabbi Yehoshua Rosenblum
58.212.264.7011

Share the **Rohr JLI** experience with friends and relatives worldwide

NOTES

NOTES

JEWISH LEARNING INSTITUTE

THE JEWISH LEARNING MULTIPLEX

Brought to you by the Rohr Jewish Learning Institute

In fulfillment of the mandate of the Lubavitcher Rebbe, of blessed memory,
whose leadership guides every step of our work,
the mission of the Rohr Jewish Learning Institute is to transform
Jewish life and the greater community through the study of Torah,
connecting each Jew to our shared heritage of Jewish learning.

While our flagship program remains the cornerstone of our organization,
JLI is proud to feature additional divisions catering to specific populations,
in order to meet a wide array of educational needs.

THE ROHR JEWISH LEARNING INSTITUTE,
a subsidiary of *Merkos L'Inyonei Chinuch*,
is the adult education arm of the Chabad-Lubavitch Movement.

TORAH STUDIES

Torah Studies provides a rich and nuanced
encounter with the weekly Torah reading.

MYSHIUR
TALMUD LEARNING INITIATIVE

MyShiur courses are designed to assist students in developing
the skills needed to study Talmud independently.

SINAI SCHOLARS SOCIETY
IN PARTNERSHIP WITH CHABAD ON CAMPUS

This rigorous fellowship program invites select college
students to explore the fundamentals of Judaism.

JLI TEENS
YOUNG SMART JEWISH

IN PARTNERSHIP WITH CTEEN: CHABAD TEEN NETWORK

Jewish teens forge their identity as they engage in
Torah study, social interaction, and serious fun.

ROSHCHODESH *society*

The Rosh Chodesh Society gathers Jewish women
together once a month for intensive textual study.

TORAHCafé

TorahCafe.com provides an exclusive selection
of top-rated Jewish educational videos.

BRILLIANT LEARNING. NATURALLY.
National JEWISH RETREAT

This yearly event rejuvenates mind, body, and spirit with
a powerful synthesis of Jewish learning and community.

the **LAND** & the **SPIRIT**
ISRAEL EXPERIENCE

Participants delve into our nation's rich past while
exploring the Holy Land's relevance and meaning today.

PEDAGOGY · CURRICULUM · MARKETING
JLI ACADEMY

Select affiliates are invited to partner with peers and noted
professionals, as leaders of innovation and excellence.

**THE SAMI ROHR
RESEARCH INSTITUTE**

Machon Shmuel is an institute providing Torah
research in the service of educators worldwide.